SOUT

● A

A TRAVELLER'S GUIDE

LITTLE HILLS PRESS

Cover photograph — courtesy Fiji Tourist Office, Sydney
Photographs by Christopher Ernest, Fay Smith, Ferdinand Kollar, Tahiti
Tourist Office, Fiji Tourist Office (cover).
Maps by Mark Butler
Typeset and Printed by Colorcraft, Hong Kong
Cover by Stuart Williams

© Little Hills Press, 1990
ISBN 0 949773 94 8

Little Hills Press Pty. Ltd.,
Tavistock House,
34 Bromham Road,
Bedford MK40 2QD,
United Kingdom.

Regent House,
37-43 Alexander Street,
Crows Nest NSW 2065 Australia.

Distributed in USA and Canada by
The Talman Company, Inc.,
150 Fifth Avenue,
New York NY 10011 USA

DISCLAIMER

Whilst all care has been taken by the publisher and editorial
team to ensure that the information is accurate and up to date,
the publisher does not take responsibility for the information
published herein. The recommendations are those of the editorial
team, and as things get better or worse, places close and others
open, some elements in the book may be inaccurate when you get
there. Please write and tell us about it so we can update in
subsequent editions.

ACKNOWLEDGEMENTS

We would like to thank the following Tourist Offices for their assistance.

Anne Green, Cook Islands Tourist Authority, Sydney.
Fiji Visitors' Bureau Office, Sydney.
New Caledonia Government Tourist Office, Sydney.
Tahiti Tourist Promotion Board, Sydney.
Tonga Visitors' Bureau, Nuku'alofa, Tongatapu.
National Tourism Office of Vanuatu, Port Vila.
Lakisa Kent, Western Samoa Visitors' Bureau, Apia.
American Samoa Office of Tourism, Pago Pago.

CONTENTS

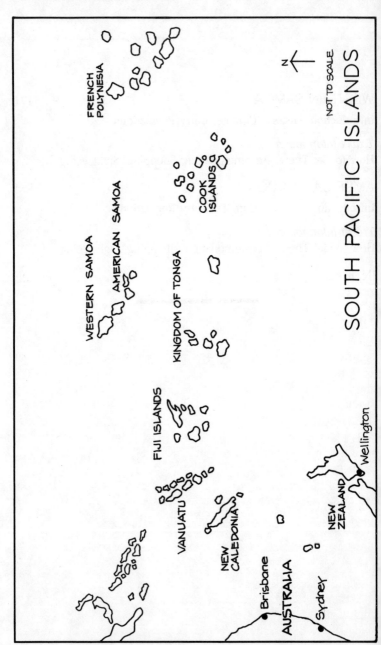

COOK ISLANDS

The islands that form the Cook Islands Group are scattered over an area of some two million square kilometres of ocean, extending from Penrhyn, 9 degrees south of the equator, to Mangaia, which is just north of the Tropic of Capricorn.

The nearest neighbours are Tahiti and Samoa. The total land area of the Cook Islands is 240 km^2 (93 sq miles) with Rarotonga's 67 km^2 (26 sq miles) the largest island, lying at the southern end of the group.

Rarotonga itself is a richly beautiful and luxuriant reef encircled island, with a rugged mountainous interior rising to 652m (2,132 ft). There is a good road circling the island which is 32 km (20 miles) in circumference.

The administrative and shopping centre is the major township of Avarua on Rarotonga.

HISTORY

While the group was named to honour the great explorer Captain James Cook (who had discovered some of the islands) the main island of Rarotonga was first sighted during the great migratory voyages of the Polynesian people during the 7th and 8th centuries.

Rarotonga was rediscovered by the Bounty Mutineers in 1789. In 1888 The Cook Islands became a British protectorate, then in 1901 a part of New Zealand. In 1965 the islands achieved self government as a dependency of New Zealand.

Members of Parliament are elected by the people, and there is a group of the main chiefs of the islands, called The Home of Ariki, which advises the government on legislation concerning customs and traditions.

The library in Avarua provides extensive reading matter on the history of the islands, and a visit is recommended.

CLIMATE

Severe weather is rare. The average temperature varies from a minimum of 18.4°C (65°F) in August, to a maximum of 29.1°C (84°F) in February. March has the highest rainfall, with 274 mm (10.8

ins) for the month. Add to that the 181 hours of sunshine recorded for March, and you might think about taking a light raincoat, but probably won't need it.

POPULATION

Of the total population of 17,200 nearly 90% live in the southern islands. Rarotonga is the most populous with some 9,281 people, followed by Aitutaki with 2,400, Mangaia 1,270, and Atiu 1,040.

Incidentally, more than 20,000 Cook Island Maoris live in New Zealand.

LANGUAGE

Cook Islands Maori is the local language, but everyone also speaks English. Here we'll give you just a taste of the local language:

Kia orana	All purpose term of greetings.
Kia Manuia	Good luck (a toast).
Meitaki	Very good — and used to say thank you.
Aere ra	Goodbye.
Maori	Polynesian person; local language.
Papa'a	European or caucasion person; English language.
Pareu	Local wrap-around sarong type garment.

PUBLIC HOLIDAYS

January 1	New Year's Day
March/April	Good Friday, Easter Monday
June	Queen's Birthday
August 4	Constitution Day
October 26	Gospel Day
December 25	Christmas Day
December 26	Boxing Day

As well as these statutory Holidays there are the following festivals and celebrations:

February	Cultural Festival Week — includes Art and Craft Display, Tivaevae (Quilt) Competition, Canoe Race.

April	Island Dance Festival Week — includes Individual Dancer of the Year Competitions
July/August	Constitution Celebration — festive and sporting activities, competition in traditional drum dance, action songs, legends, dramas and singing.
September	Cook Islands Art Exhibition Week — includes visual arts exhibition of local artists and sculptors.
October	Cook Islands Fashion Week — featuring local fashion and accessories.
November 1	All Saints Day (Taurama) –- Catholic graves are decorated with flowers and candles.
November	Tiare (Floral) Festival Week — floral float parade and flower arrangement competition.
November	Round Rarotonga Road Race.
December	Takitumu Day.

ENTRY REGULATIONS

Visitors to the Cook Islands require a current passport. Actually, New Zealand citizens do not require passports for stays of up to 31 days, but they do need one to re-enter New Zealand.

A bona-fide visitor does not require an entry permit provided he or she possesses onward passage (booked and paid for) and does not intend staying more than 31 days. (A "bona-fide" visitor is any person who enters the Cook Islands solely for the purpose of holiday or recreation and not for local employment.)

Vaccinations are not required unless arriving from an infected area.

No duty is levied on clothing or personal effects (including sports equipment). In addition, each visitor may bring the following items, duty free, into the Cook Islands.

200 cigarettes, or up to ¼ kg (½ lb) of tobacco, or up to 50 cigars, or equivalent.

2 litres of spirits or wine or 4.5 litres of beer.

2 still cameras with 24 plates or 10 rolls of film, or 1 still camera with 12 plates or 5 rolls of film and 1 miniature cine or movie camera (less than 35 mm) with 2 reels of film.

1 pair of binoculars.

1 portable record player plus 10 records.

1 portable radio.

1 portable typewriter.
1 portable musical instrument.

EMBASSIES

Australia:	No resident representative. Refer to High Commission in Wellington, NZ, ph 64 (4) 736 411.
New Zealand:	Philatelic Bureau Building, Takuvaine Road, Avarua, ph 22 201.
US:	No resident representative. Refer to Embassy in Wellington, NZ, ph 64 (4) 722 068.
UK:	No resident representative. Refer to High Commission in Wellington, NZ, ph 64 (4) 726 049.
Canada:	No resident representative. Refer to High Commission in Wellington, NZ, ph 64 (4) 739 577.

MONEY

The Cook Islands unit of currency is the New Zealand Dollar, supplemented by notes and coinage minted for local use. The dollar coin bearing the symbol of the god Tangaroa is popular with coin collectors. Local coins are not negotiable outside the Cook Islands.
Approximate exchange rates for the New Zealand Dollar are:

A$	=	NZ$1.31
US$	=	$1.60
UK£	=	$2.72
Can$	=	$1.35

COMMUNICATIONS

Mail, Telephone, Telegrams and Telex services are available through the Post Office and Cable and Wireless, who operate the island's international telecommunications. The country telephone code is 682. Internal telephone services are available at all hotels and most motels in Rarotonga.

There is a small daily newspaper containing local news which is published Monday to Saturday inclusive. There is also a weekly paper published every Friday.

Two local radio stations operate from 6 am daily, with newscasts from overseas several times a day.

MISCELLANEOUS

The Cook Islands are 10 hours behind Greenwich Mean Time — 9.5 hours during Daylight Saving. Cook Islands Time means things may take a little longer to happen here than back home, so unwind and enjoy the more relaxed pace.

Business Hours
The Westpac and Australia & New Zealand Banks in Avarua are open 9 am–3 pm Mon–Fri.
The Post Office is open weekdays, 8 am–4 pm.
Shopping hours are normally 8 am–4 pm Mon–Fri, 8 am–midday Saturday.
Some village shops are open during the evenings and on Sundays.

Voltage is 230 DC/50 cycle, the same as New Zealand and Australia. In some cases, however, a 2 pin adaptor may be required. Some hotels and motels have provision for 110 volt AC electric shavers.

There is a departure tax of NZ$20 — under 12 years NZ$10, under 2 years no tax.

The major duty-free stores, restaurants and hotels accept such credit cards as Bankcard, Visa, American Express, Mastercard and Diners Club.

As with other South Pacific locations — no bargaining or tipping.

Medical Services
Medical and dental services are available 24 hours a day.
Rarotonga has a well-equipped hospital with overseas-trained staff. There is also a pharmacy and a number of doctors in private practice.

There are no poisonous animals or insects in the Cook Islands. Mosquitoes (non-malarial) can be worrisome in inland areas, but repellants provide protection.

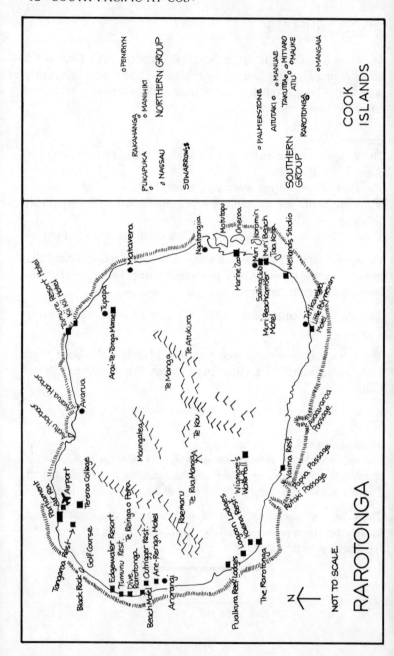

TRAVEL INFORMATION

HOW TO GET THERE

By Air
Air New Zealand have regular direct flights from New Zealand, Tahiti and Fiji, as well as connecting flights from Los Angeles, London, Tokyo and Australia.

Air Rarotonga Ltd operate a weekly service from Auckland. Cook Islands International have a weekly service from Sydney. Hawaiian Airlines operate a weekly service from Honolulu. Polynesian Airlines have a weekly service to Rarotonga from Western Samoa, with connections from Australia, New Zealand and Fiji.

The airport is on the island of Rarotonga, 4.5 km from the town centre.

TOURIST INFORMATION

Cook Islands Tourist Authority, Main Road, Avarua (P.O. Box 14, Rarotonga), ph 29 435. Open Mon–Fri, 8 am–4 pm.

ACCOMMODATION

Accommodation has to be booked in advance (it is one of the Entry Requirements) and the reason is that camping is prohibited. Also because there is not a great deal of rooms available, it would be impossible to guarantee accommodation on arrival.

Here we have divided the accommodation available into two groups — hotels/resorts and self-catered, and to give some idea of the amount of rooms available on the islands, we have put the number at each establishment in brackets. All prices are in New Zealand Dollars for twin share accommodation, and include the 10% government tax.

Hotels/Resorts

Rarotonga
Manuia Beach Hotel (20), P.O. Box 700, ph 22 461 — $159; Moana
Sands (12), P.O. Box 1007, ph 26 189 — $100; Pacific Resort (32),P.O.
Box 790, ph 20 427 — $137; Rarotonga Hotel (151), P.O. Box 103,
ph 25 800 — $159.50; Tamure Resort (35), P.O. Box 17, ph 22 415
— $60.

Aitutaki
Aitutaki Resort (25), P.O. Box 342, Rarotonga, ph 20 234 — $165;
Rapae Cottage Hotel (12), P.O. Box 79, Aitutaki, Ph 77 Aitutaki —
$65.

Self Catering

Rarotonga
Airport Lodge (16), P.O. Box 223, ph 20 050 — $28.60; Are-Renga
Motel (2), P.O. Box 223, ph 20 050 — $28.60; Ariana Bungalows (8),
P.O. Box 51, ph 20 521 — $77; Arorangi Lodges (8), P.O. Box 51, ph
27 379 — $38.50; *Dive Rarotonga Hostel (9), P.O. Box 38, ph 21 873
— $13 per person; Edgewater Resort (173), P.O. Box 121, ph 25435
— $88; Kiikii Motel (20), P.O. Box 68, ph 21 937 — $66; Lagoon
Lodges (14), P.O. Box 45, ph 22 020 — $85.80; Little Polynesian (9),
P.O. Box 366, ph 24 280 — $83.60; Mana Motel (2), P.O. Box 72, ph
26 485 — $40; *Matareka Heights (5), P.O. Box 587, ph 23 670 —
433; Muri Beachcomber (12), P.O. Box 379, ph 21 022 — $96.80;
Palm Grove (4), P.O. Box 23, ph 20 002 — $96.80; Paradise Inn (16),
P.O. Box 674, ph 20544 — $54; Puaikura Reef Lodges (12), P.O. Box
397, ph 23 537 — $73.50; Raina Beach Apartments (4), P.O. Box
1047, ph 20 197 — $80; Rarotongan Sunset (20), P.O. Box 377, ph
28 028 — $88; Sunrise Beach Motel (6), Depot 8, ph 20 417 — $88;
Tiare Village Motel (3), P.O. Box 489, ph 23 466 — $49.50;
Whitesands Motel (6), P.O. Box 115, ph 25 789 — $42.

Aitutaki
Aitutaki Lodges (6), P.O. Box 70, Aitutaki, ph 106 — $116.60;
*Aitutaki Guesthouse (4) — $38.50; *Josie's Lodge (6), Ureia — 38.50;
*Tiare Maori Guesthouse (7), Ureia — $42.90; *Tom's Beach Cottage
(8), P.O. Box 51, ph 51 — $46.

Atiu
*Atiu Motel (3), P.O. Box 79 — $60.

Mauke
*Cove Lodge (2) — $60; *Tiare Holiday Cottage (4) — $39.

*Share facilities.

LOCAL TRANSPORT

Air
Cook Islandair operate twin engined Britten-Norman Islander aircraft providing a regular air service from Rarotonga to the nearby islands of Aitutaki, Atiu, Mitiaro and Mauke.

Air Rarotonga operate Beechcraft Commuter Liner to Aitutaki, Atiu, Mauke and Mangia. Air Charter is available to all airports in the Cook Islands. Air Rarotonga also operate a Heron aircraft. Scenic flights over Rarotonga are also available.

Sea
A local shipping company operates an inter-island shipping service with frequent overnight trips to islands of the Southern Group, and a less regular service to islands in the North. Due to varying demands for cargo, timetables are not firm until a few days before departure. Details are available from the shipping company, Silk & Boyd Ltd., located at the Avatiu Wharf in Rarotonga.

Bus
Local bus companies operate an hourly service around Rarotonga from 8 am-4 pm weekdays and from 8 am–12 noon on Saturdays.

The bus stops at several hotels en route, but you can catch it anywhere along the way by hand signalling. It is a great, low-cost way to get to town, or see the sights around the island. Check the times at your hotel, or phone Circle Island Bus on 25 511.

Taxi
A number of local companies operate taxi services. Fares are government controlled and displayed in each car. Just phone for service — Kaikaveka Taxis, ph 20 213; Kapi Taxis, ph 23 510; Silver Cabs, ph 27 021; Blue Shop Taxis, ph 21 875.

Car or Motorcycle
Most hotels, motels and several companies offer cars and small motorcycles for hire. Driving in the Cook Islands is on the left-hand

side of the road. Drivers of all vehicles are required to have a current Cook Islands driver's licence, available for just $2 from the police station in downtown Avarua on presentation of your own current driver's licence, issued in your country of origin.

By the way, don't put your foot down — the maximum speed limit is 25 mph (40 km/h) in town and 30 mph (50 km/h) out of town.

Here are the phone numbers of some rental firms.

Ace Rent A Car, ph 21 901; Avis, ph 22 833; Budget Rent A Car, ph 20 888; Rental Cars (C.I.) Ltd., ph 24 442; TPA Rental Cars, ph 20 611; Tipani Rentals, ph 22 327 ext 25; Viama Rentals, ph 22 222; Kaikaveka Rentals, ph 20 213; Margaret's Hirebikes.

EATING OUT

If you plan to stay in Rarotonga for 10 days and go out every night, you still won't get around all the superb restaurants. Rarotonga offers a little of everything, from first class to friendly "islands" style cafe restaurants, and some offer courtesy transport or transfers at a nominal charge. Arrange this when you phone to make your reservations.

Make sure you see at least one Island Night during your stay. These shows feature traditional "Umukai" with the food cooked island style in an underground oven.

Another "must" is a visit to downtown Avarua and the Banana Court, which is somewhat of an institution in Rarotonga. It is the definitive nightspot of the Cooks and everyone goes there, particularly on Friday nights. If you feel like dancing to a live band, having a drink and meeting locals and other visitors, this is the place.

Try some of the traditional local foods such as ika mata (marinated fish with coconut sauce); eke (octopus); taro (tuber vegetable); rukau (spinach-like taro leaves); kun ara (sweet potato) at the Moana Cafe, Moana Sands Resort, ph 26 189 — 12.5 km from town. This cafe also serves European cuisine, and the average evening main course price ranges from $3.50 to $17.50.

You could also try the following:

Brandi's, Rarotongan Hotel, ph 25 800, International, dinner only — $19.50–$38;

Hacienda Restaurant and Bar, Cook's Corner, Avarua, ph 22 345, European, breakfast and lunch — $3.50–$5.50;

Hibiscus House Restaurant, Downtown Avarua, ph 20 823, European, lunch and dinner — $2.50-$8;

Kaena Restaurant, Arorangi, opposite Rarotongan Hotel, ph 25 433, seafood/steak, dinner only — $13-$16;

La Cantina Restaurant, 1 km from Downtown Avarua in Maraerenga, ph 29 900, Mexican/seafood/steak, lunch and dinner — $10-$18;

Mana Terrace, Rarotongan Hotel, ph 25 800, coffee shop meals, breakfast and lunch — $6-$21;

Manuia Beach Hotel, Arorangi, European/Island — $15.50-$28;

Matuas Cafe, Avarua, grills/takeaways — $8.90;

Outrigger Restaurant, Arorangi, opposite Manuia Beach Motel, ph 27 378, seafood/steak, dinner only — $16.95-$26.95;

Pacific Resort, Muri — $16;

Sizzler's, Edgewater Resort, ph 25 439, European/Island seafood — $5-$16;

PJ's, Arorangi, ph 20 367, European/Island — $11.75-$14.50;

Portofino, 1 km from Downtown Avarua in Maraerenga, ph 26 480, Italian — $13-$25;

Romiad's, Panama, ph 20 419, grills/fish/takeaways, breakfast and lunch — $5.50-$9.50;

Tangaroa Restaurant, 2 km from town at Nikae, ph 20 017, Chinese, $10.50-$15;

Tamure Resort, Tupapa, ph 22 415, European — $22-$23;

TJ's Bar/Restaurant, Avarua, seafood/Island, lunch only — $8.50-$16.50;

The Flame Tree, Muri, Asian, dinner only — $16-$24;

Tumunu Bar and Restaurant, adjacent to Edgewater Resort, ph 20 501, European/seafood, dinner only — $18-$24.90 for 2;

Vaima Restaurant, 2 km from Rarotongan Hotel, ph 26 123, local seafood/prime meat, dinner only — $16.95-$21.50;

Whitesands Restaurant, Rarotongan Hotel, ph 25 800, European/Island feasts, dinner only — $16.50-$31;

Aitutaki Resort Hotel, Aitutaki Island, a la carte/buffet/Island feasts — $27.50;

Rapae Cottage Hotel, Aitutaki Island, local foods/Island feasts — $8.50-$21.50.

SHOPPING

The main shopping area in Rarotonga is located in downtown Avarua, although there are a few shops, mostly food supplies, dotted around the island.

No bargaining is the first rule with regard to shopping in Rarotonga. Duty free goods are available at competitive prices, but the prices are fixed. Beautiful locally made handicraft (such as the traditional hats) make superb, practical souvenirs.

The Cook Islands Women's Craft Centre in downtown Avarua has especially fine examples of traditional handicrafts — particularly from the outer islands, which specialise in various products, ie finely woven mats from Pukapuka in the northern group.

Local carvings from wood and pearl shell are widely available and are good examples of the true tradition of the Cook Islands. Other popular souvenirs are colourful Cook Island stamps, available from the Philatelic Bureau (opposite the Post Office).

Be sure to inspect the natural pearls that have been cultured in the northern group of the Cook Islands, some have been handcrafted into exquisite jewellery items that are a lifetime memento of your visit to the Islands.

A unique gift to take home is the locally produced liqueurs, one of which is distilled from the pineapple in the island of Mangaia. This drink is 40% alcohol (80 proof), and if you are game there is a Free Tasting Room at the Roundabout, Downtown Avarua.

There are no glittering duty free emporiums in Rarotonga, but here we have included the names of some shops, and the merchandise they offer —

Jewellery
The Pearl Shop, Main Road Arorangi (opposite the Blue Shop), ph 21 901; Beachcomber Ltd., Cook's Corner, ph 21 939.

Duty Free
Avatiu General Traders Ltd., Main Road opposite harbour, ph 25 770; South Seas International Ltd., the Big Red Shop Downtown, ph 22 327; Linmars Duty Free and Gifts, Main Road, Avarua; Rarotonga Duty Free, CITC Building, Avarua, ph 22 000; Rarotonga Pharmacy Ltd., CITC Centre, Avarua, ph 29 292 (perfumes & cosmetics).

Island Art
The Kenwall Gallery, Ngaiekura House, Panama, Rarotonga, ph 20 477; Betela Studio of Fine Art, between Rarotongan and Arorangi, ph 25 733; Paintings by Clare Higham, ph 20 238; The Welland Studio, Muri Beach, ph 23 666.

Clothing and Handicraft
Tops'n'Bottoms Boutique, Brownes Arcade; Manu Manea, Ngaiekura House, Panama, ph 20 477; Island Craft Ltd., Centrepoint Building, Avarua; Polynesian Rakei, Cook's Corner, ph 28 223; Cook Islands Trading Corporation Ltd., the Big shop in town.

SIGHTSEEING

Local tour operators offer tours of Rarotonga and outer-island trips. For example, Union Travel, Avarua Shopping Centre in the heart of town, ph 21 780, have a Round the Island Tour, which picks up at hotels and circles Rarotonga, visiting the perfume factory, the frangi (milk) factory, Muri lagoon and the shopping centre in Avarua. They also have Across The Island Trek, which again picks up at hotels and transports you to the start of the walk, which last approximately 3.5 hours, exploring Inner Rarotonga and ascending The Needle (414 m — 1,355 ft). Their Historic Tour captures the mystery and excitement of yesteryear, visiting interesting spots off the beaten track, and relating many legends.

Stars Travel, two doors from Foodland in downtown Avarua, ph 23 669, are specialists in outer-island trips. They offer a 2 night holiday package to Aitutaki, which includes round trip airfare, accommodation, transfers and breakfast, from $203, the same to Atiu from $193, to Mauke from $195, to Mitiaro from $201. They also have an Island Combo 7 night package visiting Atiu, Mitiaro and Mauke, including round trip airfare, accommodation, some meals and transfers, from $404 per person — departures Mon, Wed and Fri.

Other tour operators with similar trips on offer are Tipani Tours, P.O. Box 4, Rarotonga, ph 22 792 and Hugh Henry & Associates, P.O. Box 440, Rarotonga, ph 25 320.

Seafari Charters Ltd., P.O. Box 148, Rarotonga, ph 20 328, have Rarotonga's biggest and best equipped charter boat, which is available for deep sea fishing, circle island cruises, sunset cruises and private charters.

Air Rarotonga, P.O. Box 79, Rarotonga, ph 22 888, have scenic flights over Rarotonga, and other package flights such as their Aitutaki Day tour which includes return flight, use of guest facilities at a resort, lunch and lagoon tour for $225 adults, $112.50 children.

RAROTONGA

Library and Museum
Open Mon–Fri 10 am–4.30 pm; Tues and Thurs 7.30–8.30 pm; Sat 8.30–11.30 am. Books can be borrowed by making arrangements with the Librarian.

Constitution Park, Victoria Road
An important venue during Constitution Celebrations. Dance competitions and other functions are held at this Park.

Wreck of the Yankee
World famous 94-foot brig Yankee ran aground on a world cruise tour at dawn on Friday July 24, 1964. No lives were lost.

Wreck of the Maitai
The SS Maitai was wrecked on December 24, 1916. This 3,393 ton vessel, owned by the Union Steam Ship Co, traded between the Cook Islands and Tahiti. No lives were lost.

Arai-Te-Tonga
These stone structures form the Koutu, chiefly courts, where the political function of the investiture of an Ariki (chief) took place. The Koutu could properly be called the royal court of a reigning Ariki or High Chief. It was a special place where all offerings to the ancient gods were first assembled prior to being conveyed to, and placed upon the Marae (meeting place) where all tribal annual feasts and the presenation of "first fruits" were held. The outstanding surviving feature of Arai-te-Tonga is a rectangular platform approx. 12 ft long, 7 ft wide and 8 ins high. Offset from the central long axis of the platform is the "Investiture Pillar", a large upright of natural squared basalt standing 7 ft above ground level.

N.B. Marae are sacred sites and should not be walked on.

Ara Metua — The Great Road of Toi
Almost circling the island is an inland road known as the Great Road

of Toi. When the first Europeans came to the Cook Islands, the Ara Metua was already there, consisting of paved stones laid through swamps to create an all-weather road. Where Toi came from is not clearly defined by legend, and why he built such a road is not known, but some archaeologists claim he built it over 1,000 years ago.

Pa's Palace

The palace of Pa (Takitumu's high chief) was built with coral and lime, indicating the central place of the village. The people of Takitumu lived inland and it was not until the missionaries built the churches that people moved to the coast.

Ngatangiia Harbour — Departure Point

A deep and relatively wide passage opening to the village from which, according to Cook Islands legend, the Great Migration of Maori Canoes (actually seven in all) departed in 1350 for New Zealand.

Wigmore's Waterfall

The only waterfall on the island is located at Vaimaanga.

Tinomana Tribe Settlement (Maungaroa Valley)

This is a four cluster settlement situated in the Maungaroa area in the village of Arorangi on the western side of the island.

Tinomana Palace

This is the second of the Tinomana Palaces built near the church when Christianity was introduced. The name of the palace is Au Maru, meaning The Peace brought by Christianity. The palace was built during the time of Enuarurutini.

Black Rock (near the Golf Course)

The original name of this place was Tuoro, meaning Welcome. According to ancient belief, this is the departure point or leaping-off point of souls. From here the souls of the deceased commenced their journey back to the fatherland, Avaiki. It is now a popular swimming place.

Stadium

Constructed for the 1985 South Pacific Mini Games, it is the first international stadium to be built in the Cook Islands, and is situated at Tereora College.

Track across the Island

A walk through rich tropical bush and a climb 306 m (1,000 ft) above sea level to reach Rarotonga's unique rock formation "The Needle". From here you have spectacular views of both sides of the island. After a short rest, it is down hill through coconut plantations to Wigmore's Waterfall. To walk the complete track, a time of 2–4 hours is estimated.

RECREATION

For the sports minded, Rarotonga offers lawn bowls, golf, tennis, squash, sailing, horse riding, snorkelling, scuba diving, wind-sailing, game fishing and mini golf.

The Rarotonga Bowling Club has an international standard bowling green and visitors are always welcome at the Saturday roll up.

Hire bowls are available — plus a licensed bar open daily from 4 pm to whenever.

The Rarotonga Sailing Club in Muri Beach, ph 27 350, is open from noon–6 pm daily except Sunday for snacks and cold ale. Canoes, surfskis, sailboards, yachts and snorkelling equipment are available for hire.

"Hash House Harriers" meet every Monday at 5.30 pm at various points for a fun run. All visitors (men, women and children) are welcome. Phone David Lobb on 22 000 (business) for information.

Tennis courts are available for hire at the Rarotonga Hotel, and you can have professional coaching to sharpen up your game. Your hotel can also advise on local courts available around the island.

The Edgewater Resort has two squash courts which can be hired, as can all the gear, ph 25 437.

At the Rarotonga Golf Club clubs can be hired for $8, and the green fees are $10 for 9 or 18 holes. Phone 27 360 for details. Saturdays are club days.

Each week there is betting on New Zealand races via the TAB at the Banana Court Bar in downtown Avarua.

Dive Rarotonga (ph 21 873) offers great value snorkelling or scuba diving excursions. This is a great place to learn and the tuition is professional and the fees are probably the lowest in the world. There is excellent deep sea fishing outside Rarotonga's sheltering reef, so contact Gamefishing — Rarotonga, ph 22 153, for details of their trips.

aboard Sea-cat. It is not a lengthy journey to the fishing areas, as they begin as soon as you leave the harbour mouth. Fishing near aggregate buoys is particularly good. Record catches at Rarotonga are in world class.

The Cook Islands Game Fishing Club, located 200 m from the Tamure Resort, 1 km from downtown, is a licensed club with 100 members, and boats for charter.

Sunday in the Cook Islands

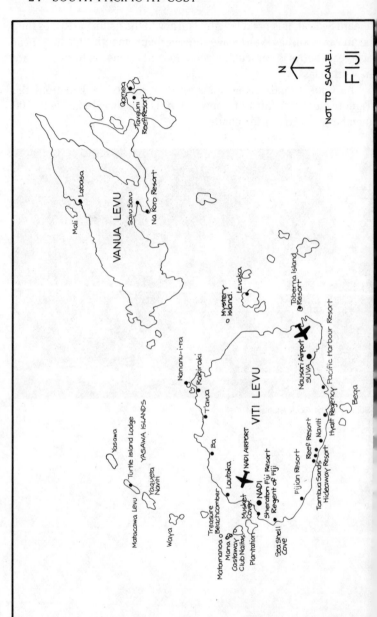

FIJI

The Fiji archipelago includes more than 300 islands scattered across some 230,000 km² (88,780 sq miles) in the south-west Pacific Ocean. Just over 100 of these islands are inhabited. Nadi International Airport is 1,710 km (1,063 miles) north-east of Sydney; 1,164 km (724 miles) north of Auckland; 2,756 km (1,713 miles) south-west of Honolulu; and 3,851 km (2,393 miles) south-east of Tokyo.

The two main islands, Viti Levu and Vanua Levu comprise 85% of the total land mass. Some of the islands are surrounded wholly or in part by coral reefs which create large lagoons and form natural harbours. The larger islands are primarily volcanic in origin with high rugged peaks that typify this type of formation. The smaller islands are mainly of coral or limestone origin.

HISTORY

Archaeologists have found pottery in Fiji which suggests that it may have been settled by Polynesians around 1500BC. Other discoveries suggest that the Melanesian people joined them about 500BC. Whatever their origins, the people engaged in continual warfare, and were extremely barbaric and cruel. They were cannibals, but even more. If they captured a particularly hated person they would chop off an ear, nose or hand, maybe cook it in front of him, and then offer him first bite. Small wonder Fiji was once known as the Cannibal Isles.

In 1643, the Dutch explorer Abel Tasman, sighted the islands but did not land. Captain Cook is credited with discovering Fiji in 1779, when he anchored off Vatoa (Turtle Island). Ten years later, when Captain Bligh was in his longboat rowing from The Mutiny to Timor, he came across Fiji and made the first chart of the area. He and his crew were chased by canoe-loads of cannibals in a section of the sea now known as Bligh Water.

The early explorers all stressed the dangers of Fiji — the warring tribes, the cannibals and the reefs surrounding the islands, and the area was shunned until 1804 when a survivor from a shipwreck realised that sandalwood grew along the coast of Vanuà Levu. This caused a rush of traders and adventurers, until they stripped the forests bare.

The first missionaries from Tonga arrived in the early 1830s, and for the next 30 years made little impact among the natives. Many of the missionaries were killed, and eaten, the last known in 1867. The first Europeans to settle were escaped convicts from Australia, who were well received as they offered to teach the Fijians how to use firearms.

The missionaries finally won through, and in 1854 the great chief, Thakombau, accepted Christianity, and in 1874 ceded his kingdom to Great Britain.

During the 1860s when the American Civil War was interfering with the world's supply of cotton, Europeans arrived in Fiji to establish cotton plantations. The first resident British governor, Sir Arthur Gordon, ruled that Fijians could not be required to work on Europeans plantations, so when it was later decided to replace cotton with sugar, Indian labour was seen as an alternative. The Indians were indentured, but after their 10-year contracts expired, many stayed on and today their descendants outnumber the native Fijians.

The British realised that the way to govern the islands was through the old chieftain system, and to protect the lands on which the system was based, ordered that native land could not be sold, only leased. Today over 80% of the land in Fiji is owned by Fijians. Approximately 12% is Crown land and the remainder is freehold.

Fiji became independent on October 10, 1970. For 17 years the Alliance Party led by Ratu Sir Kamisese Mara governed the country until elections in April 1987 toppled the Alliance. A coalition of the other two parties — the Opposition National Federation and newly formed Labour Party — ruled for a month before being dismissed in a bloodless military coup.

Fiji was declared an independent republic on September 27, 1987, and executive authority was taken over by the Head of State, President Ratu Sir Penaia Ganilau.

CLIMATE

Favoured with a warm and pleasant climate throughout the year, Fiji offers the ideal holiday destination. It enjoys a mild tropical maritime climate without extremes of hot and cold. There is a mild dry season from May to October with a warm, damp season from November to April.

POPULATION

The total population is 714,548, which comprises 46.2% Fijian, 48.6% Indian and 5.1% other races.

LANGUAGE

English, Fijian and Hindustani are the official languages, although English is generally used in Fiji.

We are not including a list of Fijian phrases as the only word you need to know is "bula", the word of greeting, and you will get to use it quite a bit.

PUBLIC HOLIDAYS

January 1	New Year's Day
March/April	Good Friday/Easter Monday
June	Queen's Birthday
August	Bank Holiday
October 10	Fiji Day
October/November	Diwali
November	Prince Charles' Birthday
December/January	Mohammed's Birthday
December 25	Christmas Day
December 26	Boxing Day

FESTIVALS

Sugar Festival — In September. The sugar city, Lautoka, comes alive with the annual festival.

Bula Festival — Nadi Town has its annual Bula Festival in July.

Diwali Festival — Held in the first half of the Hindu Month of Kartika (October/November), this is the Festival of Lights, commonly called the Diwali. Hindu homes are decorated, often elaborately, with lights.

Hibiscus Festival — Fiji's carnival of the year. Held in Suva during the month of August, the festival coincides with the first week of the school holidays.

TRADITIONS — LEGENDS

Firewalking
The unsolved mystery of how the Fijians from the Island of Beqa can walk on white-hot rocks is seen in the spectacular ritual of Fijian Firewalking. The firewalkers attribute their power to the god Veli. The Hindu ritual of firewalking is also carried out in Fiji.

The Tabua
Originally the tabuas were highly polished pieces of wood from the bua tree. When the whalers first visited Fiji, they brought ashore whales' teeth to use for trading. The Fijians were struck on the similarity of the whales' teeth to their wooden Bua-ta. The whalers named them Tabua, derived from the word "tabu" meaning sacred.

The Tabua is highly valued, not in currency, but in tradition. To be presented with one is a great honour. It is not permitted to take a Tabua out of Fiji without an export licence from the Ministry of Fijian Affairs.

Calling of The Turtles
On the island of Kadavu the maidens of the village of Namuana sing a strange chant, which brings the large sea turtles to the surface to listen to the music. This unusual phenomenon does take place and is based on an ancient legend.

Red Prawns
Legend has it that these red prawns were once a gift to the daughter of the chief of Vatulele. The daughter was so disgusted with the gift she had the prawns thrown from the cliffs. Today these sacred prawns can be found in the pools under the cliffs.

ENTRY REGULATIONS

A passport valid for at least three months beyond the length of stay is required. On arrival a temporary visa is issued valid for 30 days, provided you have an onward ticket to a country you are authorised to enter, and proof of sufficient funds for your up-keep in Fiji. Vaccinations are not required unless entering from a designated infected area.

The duty free allowance is:

200 cigarettes, or 250 gm of cigars, or 250 gm of tobacco or all three
  but not exceeding 250 gm altogether.
1 litre of liquor or 2 litres of wine or 2 litres of beer.
Up to F$50 per passenger of any duty assessed goods.

EMBASSIES

Australia: Australian High Commission, Dominion House,
                 Thomson Street, Suva, ph 312 844.
New Zealand: NZ High Commission, Reserve Bank of Fiji Building,
                 Pratt Street, Suva, ph 311 422.
US: US Embassy, 31 Loftus Street, Suva, ph 314 446.
UK: British High Commission, Victoria House, 47
                 Gladstone Road, Suva, ph 311 033.
Canada: No resident representative. Refer to High Commis-
                 sion in Wellington, NZ, ph 64 (4) 739 577.

MONEY

The basic unit of currency is the Fijian dollar. Notes come in
denominations of $1, $2, $5, $10, $20, and coins are 1c, 2c, 5c, 10c,
20c, 50c. Approximate exchange rates are:

A$	=	F$1.17
NZ$	=	$0.90
US$	=	$1.43
UK£	=	$2.45
Can$	=	$1.20

COMMUNICATIONS

Fiji's telecommunications system is administered by the Department
of Posts and Telecommunications (P&T) in cooperation with Fiji
International Telecommunications Limited (FINTEL). International
Direct Dialling is available and the country code is 679.

   Outer islands in the Fiji group not on the direct phone lines are
serviced by a radio telephone system.

   Public telephones take 10c coins for local calls and can be
found at all post offices.

   There are two English language daily Newspapers, Fiji Times
and the Fiji Sun.

   Fijian and Hindustani language newspapers are published weekly.

MISCELLANEOUS

Local time is GMT + 12.

Business Hours
Banks: 10 am–3 pm Mon–Fri, 10 am–4 pm Fri. Bank of New Zealand operates a 24 hour service at Nadi International Airport.
Post Offices: 8 am–4.30 pm Mon–Fri, 8 am–11 am Sat.
Government Offices: 8 am–4.30 pm Mon–Thurs, 8 am–4 pm Fri, closed for lunch.
Commercial outlets, including the vegetable and handicraft markets, are open five days a week and Saturday morning. They do not usually close for lunch. There is minimal commercial activity in the cities and towns on Sundays and Public Holidays.

Electricity is 240 volts, 50 cycles AC. Most hotels have 110 volt converters for razors. Electrical outlets accept the three prong, angled configuration plug, like those used in Australia and New Zealand. Adaptors can be purchased from electrical suppliers in most towns and cities.

There is a F$10 departure tax.

Credit Cards are widely accepted.

Tipping is not compulsory in Fiji, but you may want to give a gratuity for excellent service, or contribute to a staff Christmas fund.

Medical
Fiji is free from most tropical diseases including malaria. Drinking water is safe in all cities, resorts and urban areas.
   Hospitals are located in Suva, Sigatoka, Lautoka, Ba, Savusavu, Taveuni, Labasa and Levuka.
   Most small towns and built up areas have a government clinic staffed by a District Nurse and assistants.
   There is a minimal charge for patients who are not citizens of Fiji. Private medical services are available.

Emergency Telephone Numbers

Fire — Suva	22 688
Police — Suva	311 222
Ambulance — Suva	313 444
Emergency	000

TRAVEL INFORMATION

HOW TO GET THERE

By Air

Air Pacific have regular flights from Brisbane, Sydney, Melbourne, Christchurch, Honiara, Tonga, Apia, Tokyo, Port Vila, to Nadi, and from Tonga and Apia to Suva.

Qantas flights all arrive at Nadi, and come from Honolulu, Brisbane, Melbourne, Sydney, San Francisco, Los Angeles, New York and Vancouver.

Canadian Airlines have services to Nadi from Auckland, Brisbane, Sydney, Honolulu, Los Angeles, New York and Vancouver.

Air New Zealand flies to Nadi from Auckland, Christchurch, Los Angeles via Hololulu, Sydney, Vancouver, London via Los Angeles, Papeete via Rarotonga, Tokyo and Frankfurt.

By Sea

Passenger lines serving Fiji are Royal Viking Line, Sitmar, P & O, Princess Cruises, CTC Cunard, Norwegian America and Polish Ocean.

TOURIST INFORMATION

Fiji Visitors' Bureau has its head office in Thomson Street, Suva, ph 22 867. It also has an office at Nadi Airport, ph 72 433.

There are a number of tourist related publications which appear regularly.

The Fiji Beach Press and Fiji Fantastic, published weekly, provide up-to-date tourist information, and are distributed free through hotels and Fiji Visitors' Bureau offices.

Other useful publications include: Talanoa (quarterly), Fiji Today (Ministry of Information, bi-monthly), Islands Business (monthly), Discover Fiji (every six months by News South Pacific).

ACCOMMODATION

There is no shortage of accommodation in Fiji, the only problem is making up your mind what type of accommodation to choose — international standard resort, large town hotel, island resort or bure (Fijian native house) accommodation. Here we list some examples, with prices for a twin room in Fijian dollars, which should be used as a guide only.

Nadi

The Regent of Fiji, P.O. Box 441, Nadi — $167–207; Sheraton Fiji Resort, P.O. Box 9761, Nadi Airport, ph 71 777 — $165–205; Fiji Mocambo, P.O. Box 9195, Nadi Airport, ph 72 000 — $110–120; Nadi Airport Travelodge, P.O. Box 9203, Nadi Airport, ph 72 277 — $98.

Tanoa Hotel, P.O. Box 9211, Nadi Airport, ph 72 300 — $85; Castaway Gateway Hotel, P.O. Box 9246, Nadi Airport, ph 72 444 — $70–88; Dominion International Hotel, P.O. Box 9178, Nadi Airport, ph 72 255 — $60; Skylodge Hotel, P.O. Box 9222, Nadi Airport, ph 72 200 — $58; Seashell Cove Resort, P.O. Box 9530, Nadi Airport, ph 72 900 — $50.

Nadi Hotel, P.O. Box 91, Nadi, ph 70 000 — $26–50; Seashell Cove Resort Ltd., P.O. 9530, Nadi Airport, ph 72 900 — $45; Travellers Beach Resort, P.O. Box 700, Nadi, ph 73 322 — $30–45; Sandalwood Inn, P.O. Box 445, Nadi, ph 72 553 — $26–38; Nadi Sunseekers Hotel, P.O. Box 100, Nadi, ph 70 400 — $20–35; Fong Hing Hotel, P.O. Box 143, Nadi, ph 71 011 — $24.

Island Resorts, Nadi Area

Matamanoa Island Resort, P.O. Box 9729, Nadi Airport, ph 60 511 — $150, bure sleeps 6; Mana Island Resort, P.O. Box 610, Lautoka, ph 61 333 — $135, bure; Castaway Island Resort, P.O. Box 9246, Nadi Airport, ph 61 233 — $127, bure sleeps 4; Musket Cove Resort, Private Mail Bag, Nadi Airport, ph 62 215 — $108–120, incl. airfare from Nadi; Club Naitasi, P.O. Box 9147, Nadi Airport, ph 72 352 — $110.

Lautoka

Plantation Island Resort, P.O. Box 9176, Nadi Airport, ph 72 333 — $145–195; Navini Island Resort, P.O. Box 685, Lautoka, ph 62 188 — $114–142, bure; Beachcomber Island Resort, P.O. Box 364, Lautoka,

Games in the South Pacific

Catholic Cathedral, Nuku'alofa, Tonga

One way to get around Viti Levu, Fiji

ph 61 500 — $125-150 includes meals; Musket Cove Resort, Private Mail Bag, Nadi Airport, ph 62 215 — $88-120 incl. airfare from Nadi; Treasure Island, P.O. Box 364, Lautoka, ph 61 599 — $140, bure; Cathay Hotel, P.O. Box 239, Lautoka, ph 60 566 — $16-22.

Coral Coast
The Fijian Resort, Private Mail Bag, Nadi Airport, ph 50 155 — $135-170; Hyatt Regency Fiji, P.O. Box 100, Korolevu, ph 50 555 — $105-164; Castaway Naviti Resort, P.O. Box 29, Korolevu, ph 50 444 — $127; Fiji Palms Beach Club Resort, Postal Agency, Pacific Harbour, ph 45 050 — $105, apartment sleeps 3-4; Casablanca Beach Hotel, P.O. Box 164, Sigatoka, ph 50 766 — $70-90; Tambua Sands Beach Resort, P.O. Box 177, Sigatoka, ph 50 399 — $72-84, bure for 4-5; Reef Resort, P.O. Box 173, Sigatoka, ph 50 044 — $80; Crow's Nest, P.O. Box 270, Sigatoka, ph 50 230 — $75-85; Hideaway Resort, P.O. Box 233, Sigatoka, ph 50 177 — $66, bure for 3, $85, bure for 5; Man Friday Resort, P.O. Box 20, Korolevu, ph 50 185 — $65.

Deuba
Pacific Harbour Villas, Postal Agency, Pacific Harbour, ph 45 022 — $110-220, villa; Fiji Palms Beach Club Resort, Postal Agency, Pacific Harbour, ph 45 050 — $105, apartment for 304; Pacific Harbour International Resort, Postal Agency, Pacific Harbour, ph 45 022 — $90.

Suva
Suva Travelodge, P.O. Box 1357, Suva, ph 314 600 — $105-115; Suva Courtesy Inn, P.O. Box 112, Suva, ph 312 300 — $75; Southern Cross Hotel, P.O. Box 1076, Suva, ph 314 233 — $54; Townside Apartment Hotel, P.O. Box 485, Suva, ph 22 661 — $42-50; Tropic Towers Apartment Hotel, P.O. Box 1347, Suva, ph 25 819 — $28-45; Sunset Apartment Motel, P.O. Box 485, Suva, ph 23 021 — $38-40; Grand Pacific Hotel, P.O. Box 2086, Government Buildings, Suva, ph 23 011 — $35-45; Suva Peninsula Hotel, P.O. Box 888, Suva, ph 313 711 — $38; Sunseekers Outrigger Apartment Hotel, P.O., Box 750, Suva, ph 313 563 — $30-35; Pacific Grand Apartments, P.O. Box 875, Suva, ph 25 583 — $21, apartment for 3; South Seas Private Hotel, P.O. Box 157, Suva, ph 22 195 — $11.

Island Resort, Suva Area
Toberua Island Resort, P.O. Box 567, Suva, ph 49 177 — $212.

Rakiraki Area, Tavua-Ba

Rakiraki Hotel, P.O. Box 31, Rakiraki, ph 94 101 — $55; Ba Hotel, P.O. Box 29, Ba — $30; Tavua Hotel, P.O. Box 4, Tavua, ph 91 122 — $18-28; Nananu Beach Cottages, P.O. Box 140, Rajkiraki, ph 22 672 — $30, cottage.

Labasa — Savusavu

Na Koro Resort, P.O. Box 12, Savusavu, ph (86) 188 — $190; Kontiki Lodge, P.O. Box 244, ph 86 262 — $150, bure; Savusavu Hot Springs Hotel, P.O. Box 208, Savusavu, ph 86 111 — $55-75; Coral Island Resort, Island of Nukubati, P.O. Box 7 Labasa — $45-70, bure; Hotel Takia, P.O. Box 7, Labasa, ph 81 655 — $38-46.

Outer Islands

Qamea Beach Club, P.O. Box Matei, Tavenui, ph 87 220 — $210, bure; Maravu Plantation Resort, Postal Agency Matei Taveuni, ph 401A (Taveuni) — $110, bure; Moody's Namena, Private Mail Bag, Suva, ph 906 388, via operator 81 010 — $110, bure; Matagi Island, P.O. Box 83, Waiyevo, Taveuni, ph (Taveuni 87) 260 — $65; Mystery Island Resort, P.O. Box 12539, Suva, ph 44 364 — $60; Rukuruku Holiday Resort, P.O. Box 112, Levuka, ph Suva 312 507 — $35, bure; Turtle Island, P.O. Box 9317, Nadi Airport, ph 72 921 — rates on application, bure.

Cruising

Blue Lagoon Cruises, P.O. Box 54, Lautoka, ph 61 622, 61 268 — $270-644 4 day/3 night cruise — $545-1378 7 day/6 night cruise.

LOCAL TRANSPORT

Bus

There is an extensive bus service on most of Fiji's main islands. Scheduled services in air conditioned coaches are operated by: Tradewinds Tours (Queens Coach) between Lautoka and Suva. Pacific Transport Company between Lautoka and Suva. United Touring Company (UTC) between Nadi Airport and the Hyatt Regency Fiji.

Bus service is provided for airline passengers between Air Pacific's sales office in Suva and Nausori Airport.

Most visitors on package tours are provided with airport and hotel transfers in very comfortable coaches operated by UTC, Sun Tours,

Tapa Tours, Yanuca Tours, Fiji Tours, Tradewinds Tours, Tourist Transport (Fiji) Ltd. and Nausori Bus and Taxi Service.

Taxi
Most towns and cities have taxi stands. All taxis are metered and charges of 30c flag fall plus 40c for every kilometre within town or city limits is standard. For longer trips a price should be agreed upon beforehand.

Car
Overseas driving licences and international driving permits are recognised in Fiji for a maximum period of six months after arrival.

Driving is on the left hand side of the road, although in the small towns and villages the locals tend to drive in the middle of the road, and it seems they also consider the most important part of a car to be the horn which they use frequently.

Roads in the main cities and towns are for the most part sealed (paved). Several of the highways on Fiji's main island of Viti Levu are also sealed.

There is a wide selection of rental car agencies in Fiji, and here we have listed some.

Avis Rent-A-Car, P.O. Box 9088, Nadi Airport, ph 72 688; A-Team Rentals, P.O. Box 9028, Nadi Airport, ph 73 100; Budget Rent A Car, P.O. Box 12170, Suva, ph 315 899, Nadi Airport, ph 72 735; Hertz Rental Car, P.O. Box 420, Suva, ph 23 206; Khan's Rental Cars Ltd., P.O. Box 299, Nadi, ph 71 009; National Car Rentals, P.O. Box 9101, Nadi Airport, ph 72 740, Suva, ph 311 677; Bula Rentals, P.O. Box 9268, Nadi Airport, ph 70 710; Pauls Rentals, P.O. Box 7, Labasa, ph 81 004; Roxy Rentals, P.O. Box 9529, Nadi Airport, ph 70 710; Thrifty Car Rentals, P.O. Box 9268, Nadi Airport, ph 72 935; UTC Rent A Car, P.O. Box 9172, Nadi Airport, ph 72 811.

Ship
John Lum On Shipping, P.O. Box 866, Suva, ph 381 727. The MV Gurawa departs from Princess landing, Suva, for Ono in northern Kadavu and Nakasaleka twice a week. Each trip takes 3 days.

Kaunitoni Shipping Co Ltd (Marine Department), P.O. Box 326, Suva, ph 312 668. Check with agent for departure details. Departs from Suva for the Lau Group. Takes 8–9 days for Northern and Central Lau, 9–10 days for Southern Lau (weather permitting).

Wong's Shipping Co Ltd, P.O. Box 1269, Suva, ph 311 888, 311 741, 311 867. Ships: Tovata, Belama and Evelyn sail to Koro, Gau and Savusavu — 4 days. Also to Kadavu ports — 4 days. Belama and Tovata sail to Taveuni, Laucala, Kanacea and Naitauba, Mago, Cicia, Lakeba and Vanua Balavu ports. Takes 7–10 days.

Paterson Bros Shipping Co Ltd, Suite 1 & 2 Epworth House, Nina Street, Private Mail Bag, Suva, ph 315 644. Ferry services between Natovi, Levuka, Nobouwalu and Suva.

North West Shipping Co, P.O. Box 5312, Raiwaqa, Suva, ph 385 388. Ferry services between Suva, Levuka, Koro, Taveuni, Savusavu and Kadavu.

Consort Shipping Line Ltd, P.O. Box 152, Suva, ph 313 344, 311 888. Ferry services between Suva, Koro and Savusavu.

EATING OUT

The resort hotels offer a varied menu that usually features European cuisine, Fijian and Indian dishes. Fiji's major towns offer a respectable choice of restaurants and cafes. Indian curry houses and cafes serving Fijian food offer a choice of tasty local foods. You can also choose from Chinese, Italian, French, European and Japanese restaurants depending upon the region of Fiji.

The bigger towns and cities abound with things to do at night, from cinemas to nightclubs and restaurants. In addition, on weekends there are usually dances. Check the classified section of the local newspapers, the Fiji Beach Press and Fiji Fantastic, or ask at your hotel about evening activities.

There are licensed restaurants, clubs and hotels throughout Fiji that offer a wide range of liquors and wines. Carlton Brewery (Fiji) Ltd, located in Suva and Lautoka, brew Fiji Bitter beer. Local wine, Meridian Moselle and Suvanna Moselle, are also available. South Pacific Distilleries produce Old Club Whisky, Booth's Gin, Cossack Vodka, Bounty OP Rum, Bounty White Rum, Regal Whisky, Regal Gin, Gin Beam Whisky, Bardinet Brandy and Ratu's Plantation Rum.

Lovo
The "lovo" is a traditional Fijian feast in which food is wrapped in

banana leaves and cooked slowly in an earth oven over smouldering stones. A distinctive faintly smoke flavour can be tasted in the food. Vegetables, fish and meats are placed in the earthen oven. Many of the dishes are prepared in coconut milk. The centrepiece of the lovo is often a whole pig.

Yaqona (Kava)
Throughout Fiji, and in most parts of Polynesia, the drinking of Yaqona (pronounced Yanggona) or Kava, is a common ceremonial and social custom. Yaqona is made from the root of the pepper plant, Piper methysticum. The yaqona ceremony is still important in the Fijian way of life. Today it has become a social custom as well as ceremonial.

In old Fiji, birth, marriage and death, the installation of chiefs, welcoming of important visitors, launching of canoes, and when a chief of rank visited another village all called for the traditional Yaqona ceremony. Many of these same ceremonies are still performed today. When you are offered a bowl (bilo) the correct procedure is to clap twice, take the coconut bowl and drink all the yaqona at once. Be warned, though, it looks like dirty creek water, doesn't taste much better, and your lips become numb.

SHOPPING

Fiji has developed a major duty free shopping industry. Electrical and sports equipment, appliances, jewellery, porcelain, perfume, cosmetics, cameras and accessories are just a few of the products available at greatly reduced prices. Major brand name products are available.

Duty free shopping outlets can be found in cities, towns and hotels. Check the local newspapers or contact the Fiji Visitors' Bureau offices for a complete listing.

Bargaining is still conducted in some duty free shops.

Resort wear and local fashions can be found at shops and resorts. These include sulus, bula shirts for men and a variety of swimwear.

Tailors, of which there are many, make quality men's and women's fashions in a few days.

Dress lengths are an excellent buy in Fiji at reasonable prices.

SIGHTSEEING

GENERAL

The Fiji Islands are a tropical paradise of white sandy beaches, coconut palms, warm sea breezes, and clear blue waters and lagoons. The islands are fringed with coral reefs that teem with sea life.

The larger islands contain steep sided volcanic mountains covered with tropical rainforests. Jungles reveal fast flowing streams cascading into clear pools. They do not have poisonous spiders or snakes, and the most common "wild beast" is the noisy but harmless flying fox.

The smaller coral islands are havens for birds and turtles amidst coconut trees.

VITI LEVU

Fiji's principal island, comprising 10,429 km^2 (4,026 sq miles), is home of the country's capital city, Suva. The majority of Fiji's hotels and resorts are located on this island. It is the primary location for the main industries of sugar, tourism, timber and gold, and most of the country's population lives here. It has two deep water ports, one in Lautoka and the other in Suva, two International Airports located at Nadi and Nausori, and Fiji's greatest urban development at Suva, Nausori, Navua, Sigatoka, Nadi, Lautoka, Ba and Rakiraki.

Nadi (pronounced Nandee)

Situated on the west coast of Viti Levu, Nadi is the site of Fiji's primary International Airport and the main point of entry for the majority of visitors. The area is also the home of, or gateway to, the most popular tourist hotels and resorts, including the popular offshore resorts of the Mamanuca Island Group.

Nadi is mainly a one street town, with not much in the way of sights, except for a couple of mosques. Its main attraction is its duty free shops, which are lined up side by side from one end of town to the other.

Suva

The capital of Fiji is situated in the south-eastern corner of Viti Levu, and is very much a multi-racial town. It is well known for its duty free shopping, and has some very good markets. Although you might not be interested in buying fruit and vegetables, fish or meat, the markets near the wharves are well worth a visit for the local colour and atmosphere.

A short walk from there along Stinson Parade is the Handicrafts Centre. This is not the government run handicrafts shop, which is on Carnarvon Street, but is where the locals do their shopping, so here you really have to bargain hard to get that special souvenir.

Even in the main street, Victoria Parade, it is important to watch out for touts, and if someone asks your name, just ignore them, for if you tell them you will be presented with a wooden "sword" with your name scratched on it and be asked to pay some ridiculous price for it. This can turn nasty, especially if the "salesman" happens to be (as they usually are) a very large, well-muscled native.

You can see the whole of Suva by foot, even if you are not an extremely energetic person, but do remember to take an umbrella because it is a very wet town.

Sigatoka
Situated at the mouth of the Sigatoka River, Fiji's second longest river, Sigatoka is a small town with a very good market, and many duty free shops. Actually it is much more pleasant shopping here for your duty free goods than in the hustle and bustle of Nadi or Suva.

Lautoka
Lautoka is 19 km north of Nadi, and has Fiji's largest sugar mill (conducted tours June–December). Most of the cruise lines include Lautoka in their itineraries, but be warned, the prices at the local markets rise considerably when there is a cruise ship in port.

This is also the departure point for Blue Lagoon Cruises (3–7 days to Yasawa Islands) and Island in the Sun Cruises (daily to Beachcomber Island).

Lautoka also has its fair share of duty free ships, but its main interest is sugar rather than tourism, and for that reason alone it is worth a visit.

VANUA LEVU

The country's second largest island, comprising 5,556 km (2,2145 sq miles), is located north of Viti Levu. At one time it was the centre of the sandalwood trade, but now its primary economy is sugar and copra. Its main port is Savusavu. The principal urban centre is Labasa, which also has a small port and the island's main airport.

Comfortable visitor accommodation is available in Labasa and Savusavu.

TAVEUNI

Known as the Garden Island, this is the country's third largest island, and boasts lush vegetation, spectacular waterfalls, miles of sand beaches and the country's national flower, the legendary Tagimoucia. Its primary economy is copra, with tourism playing a dominant role. A major leisure development is located at Soqulu, with a comfortable resort hotel nearby. It is easily reached by air.

KADAVU

Accessible by boat and air, this island has one of the finest scuba diving locations in the world, the Great Astrolabe. The economy, like most of the island group is built around copra.

LOMAIVITI

This group of islands is located to the east of Viti Levu and includes Ovalau and the private island of Wakaya, which is famous for its wild deer. There is very little visitor traffic to these islands, with the exception of Ovalau. There are airfields on Koro and Gau, with a private landing strip on Wakaya.

LAU GROUP

These islands form the eastern section of Fiji. The most famous is Lakeba, the traditional home of the Tui Nayau, the country's Prime Minister, Ratu Sir Kamisese Mara.

The economy is based exclusively on copra. There are virtually no tourists although a guest house has been opened on one of the islands in the group. There are airports on Lakeba, Vanuabalavu, Moala, Cicia and Ono-i-Lau. Yachts wishing to call at Lau must first receive permission from the Secretary of Fijian Affairs at the Native Land Trust Board Building in Suva.

THE YASAWAS

The western most islands in the Fijian chain, they remain only slightly influenced by the outside world with no airport and no regular inter-island transportation. The islands have become better known because of Blue Lagoon Cruises, who offer four and seven day cruises through the islands. They have magnificent mountain scenery, isolated beaches and limestone formations. The limestone caves at Sawa-i-Lau with their ancient wall writings are worth a visit.

THE MAMANUCAS

A chain of islands visible on a clear day from Nadi, they have often been called The Mecca of Fiji. Many of the outer-island resorts are located in this group. They are considered to be among the most scenic islands in the country.

OVALAU

Located off the eastern side of Viti Levu, this island is the home of the old capital of Fiji, Levuka. This was the sight of the Deed of Cession in 1874, and the waterfront of the old capital looks much as it did a century ago. There are small guest houses, hotels and a port. The centre of Fiji's fishing industry, complete with fish canning factory, is located at Levuka. A road circles the island linking villages with the airport at Bureta and the town of Levuka.

BAU

A small island located off Viti Levu, this is the home of the Paramount Chief of Fiji, and also the former Governor-General, Ratu Sir George Cakobau whose grandfather ceded the Fiji Islands to Great Britain.

ORGANISED TOURS

LAUTOKA AND NADI

A wide range of organised tours are available. Half-day reef cruises, scenic drives, game fishing or scuba diving expeditions are but a few. Most bookings and further information is readily available at hotel tour desks or through travel agents.

Vuda Look-Out Tour
Half-day tour. Travel in a northerly direction through the mountainous Sabeto Valley. Visit a Muslim mosque. Continue on to the Viseisei Village where Fijians first landed, then on to the Vuda Lookout where there is a panoramic view of the Vuda Valley, Nadi Airport and surrounding island resorts. Departs Nadi twice daily. For further information — Road Tours of Fiji Limited, P.O. Box 9268, Nadi Airport, ph 72 935.

Waqadra Garden Tour
While in Nadi take a half day tour to the Waqadra Garden and stroll through a 70-year-old tropical, botanical garden that surrounds an old

family homestead plantation. Refreshments will be served while on the tour. For bookings — ph 72 344.

Garden of the Sleeping Giant
Started by Raymond Burr (of Perry Mason fame) in 1977 to house his private Fiji orchid collection, it is now open to the public. The Garden houses the largest, most varied orchid collection in Fiji. It also contains an unusually wide variety of flowering tropical plants and trees. Open from 9 am to sunset, visitors are welcome to explore on their own, or with guides. For bookings — Garden of the Sleeping Giant, P.O. Box 9447, Nadi Airport, ph 72 701.

Nausori Highlands
This is an adventure tour into the centre of the island, through farmlands, mountain passes to a lush rain forest in the heart. It passes ornate mosques and fields of sugarcane on the way to Nausori range, which has spectacular views of Nadi Bay and the offshore islands. The highlight is a visit to one of the villages for refreshments. Tour leaves from hotels in the Nadi area twice daily. For information — Scenic Tours of Fiji, P.O. Box 9023, Nadi Airport, ph 73 368.

Seaplane Sightseeing
Operates daily from Newtown Beach, Nadi to Nadi Bay resorts (Mana, Castaway, Treasure, Beachcomber, Plantation, Musket Cove and Club Naitasi). 10-15 minutes flight only. Leave anytime from sunrise to sunset for sightseeing. Charters throughout Fiji can be arranged. Schedules 24 hours beforehand to suit your time as close as possible. Bookings — Turtle Airways, P.O. Box 718, Nadi, ph 72 988.

Pacific Harbour Cultural Centre and Marketplace.
Full day tour. Departs Nadi daily except Sunday. Tour drives through the sugarcane plantations to the new pine forests (Fiji's green gold), then past villages, palm fringed beaches and Sigatoka township for the morning tea stop at the Tambua Sands Hotel. After this leisurely break it is on to Pacific Harbour and a tour of the International Resort before lunch at the golf course clubhouse (price not included). Then comes the highlight, the Cultural Centre and Marketplace. Even visitors who have become quite blase about "cultural" exhibitions will find this place fascinating. It contains really good speciality shops, and the gardens and the island village are beautiful. Time is your own until 4.30 pm when the tour departs Pacific Harbour for the return

journey to Nadi. For further information — Road Tours of Fiji Ltd, P.O. Box 9268, Nadi Airport, ph 72 935.

Although this particular tour leaves from Nadi, the Cultural Centre is actually less than half an hour's drive from Suva along the Queens Highway. If you have your own transport this would be the better starting off point. Allow a few hours for your visit, and make sure you see the entire cultural show, which includes fire-walking, in my experience, the best in the South Pacific.

Fiji Trekking and Camping Safari

A 4 day/3 night tour which explores the rugged beauty of the island of Viti Levu. It begins at Nadarivatu in the highlands and works its way down to the upper reaches of the Sigatoka River, visiting isolated Fijian villages. All equipment is designed and tested to ensure that your adventure trek is a comfortable safari, especially at day's end. Recommended age group between 15 and 50. The trekking and camping safari operates with a minimum of 4 persons, but up to a group of 15 could be handled. Departs once a week. For information and bookings — Wilderness Adventures (Fiji) Limited, P.O. Box 1389, Suva, ph 313 500.

"Sereki Mai" Private Charter Cruises

The 48ft motor cruiser "Sereki Mai" based at Navini Island Resort is available for private charter throughout the Mamanuca and Yasawa Islands. Day trips through the Mamanucas — minimum 20 people. For Yasawa cruises of 2-6 days, accommodation onboard is for five guests in two private cabins, plus the use of two traditional Fijian bures at an exclusive Manuka bay anchorage in the Yasawas. Fishing, snorkelling, beachcombing on uninhabited islands, cave exploring, village visits — all at leisure. All meals included and there are bar facilities on board. For information and bookings — Navini Island Resort, P.O. Box 685, Lautoka, ph 62 188.

Beachcomber Day Cruise

Departs Lautoka wharf daily at 10 am for Beachcomber Island Resort. Courtesy bus pick-up and return from all Nadi and Lautoka hotels. Sail on the vessels "Tui Tai", "Ratu Bulumakau", "Adriane" or "Viti". There is a licensed bar on the vessels, and fresh local fruit in season is served on board. Buffet lunch is served on the island. Departs Beachcomber Island at 4 pm and arrives Lautoka wharf at 5.15 pm.

Further information — Islands in The Sun (Fiji) Ltd, P.O. Box 364, Lautoka, ph 61 500.

Fiji Skypark Tour
A half-day tour which goes to Viseisei Village on Vuda Point, the oldest village in Fiji, then a ten minute drive up to 1200 ft and the "skypark" from which a panoramic view of Nadi Bay, Lautoka and the interior of Viti Levu is obtained. Then on to the Garden of the Sleeping Giant. The tour operates daily except Sunday and picks up at 1.30 pm from Nadi area hotels. Return is at approximately 5.30 pm. For reservations — United Touring Fiji Ltd, P.O. Box 9172, Nadi Airport, ph 72 811.

Sara Sara Fiji Tour
A full-day tour which picks up from Nadi and Coral Coast hotels at 7.30 am and returns at approximately 7.30 pm. After a tour of the Pacific Harbour complex, there is a visit to the Cultural Centre and marketplace, with an island village tour in a sheltered canoe. After lunch there is entertainment either by the Fijian Firewalkers of Yanuca (Tuesday) or the Dance Theatre of Fiji (Thursday and Saturday). After the show there is time to browse through the duty free shopping arcade within the Market Place. Operates Tuesday, Thursday and Saturday. For reservations — United Touring Fiji Ltd, P.O. Box 9172, Nadi Airport, ph 72 811.

Bula Fiji Tour — Suva Guided Day Tour
Tour operates Monday through Friday (subject to confirmation). Pick-up is at 7.30 am from Nadi and Coral Coast Hotels. Airconditioned coach tour includes — island village tour at the Cultural Centre and Market Place at Pacific Harbour, Suva city drive, Museum visit and shopping in Suva City. Tour departs Suva at 4 pm. Information and bookings — United Touring Fiji Limited, P.O. Box 9172, Nadi Airport, ph 72 811, or Suva, ph 25 637.

Explore Fiji Tour — Cannon Route
One of the most exciting guided tours offered. Operates daily except Sundays. Morning pick-up from Nadi Airport hotels in air-conditioned coach. First stop is Waqadra Gardens, then on to Momi Gun Batteries, an historical landmark with a panoramic view of Mamanuca Islands. Nearby Sheashell Cove Resort is provided as a convenience stop. Tour includes a visit to the interesting village of Tau which is rich in

folklore and tradition. Further information — United Touring Fiji Ltd, P.O. Box 9172, Nadi Airport, ph 72 811.

Mana Island Day Cruise

Departs daily from the Regent of Fiji aboard the 25 m catamaran cruiser "Island Express". Coach pick-up Nadi area hotels from 8 am for 9 am departure from the Regent, with arrival at Mana at 10.35 am. On the island there is swimming, snorkelling, shelling, water skiing, etc and a BBQ/smorgasbord lunch. For information — South Sea Cruises, P.O. Box 718, Nadi Airport, ph 72 988.

Round Fiji Coach Tour

A five-day escorted tour departs Nadi once a week and drives along the coast road to the Sugar City of Lautoka. From there to the towns of Ba, Tavua and Rakiraki, with overnight at Rakiraki Hotel. Next morning its off to Suva with two nights accommodation at the Southern Cross Hotel. Departs for the Coral Coast on the 4th day. Accommodation at the Naviti Beach Resort. On the 5th day its the drive back to Nadi. For reservations — United Touring Fiji Ltd, P.O. Box 9172, Nadi Airport, ph 72 811.

4 Island Sightseeing Trip

Half day cruise aboard the "Island Express". Coach pick-up from Nadi area hotels at 8 am and 12.45 pm. Return transport is provided. Boat departs the Regent of Fiji at 9 am and 1.30 pm. A four hour cruise to four well known island resorts off Nadi. Facilities onboard include licensed, air-conditioned lounge bar, coffee shop and shopping boutique. Bookings — South Sea Cruises, P.O. Box 718, Nadi Airport, ph 72 988.

Magic Island Day Cruise

Departs the Regent of Fiji beach at 9.30 am aboard 86 ft schooner "Seaspray", of television fame, to uninhabited Magic Island on Plantation Island Barrier Reef. Coral viewing, fishing, snorkelling gear and lunch provided. Bar taken ashore. No resort guests — the island is all yours. The "Seaspray" arrives back at the Regent beach at 3.30 pm. Bookings — South Sea Cruises, P.O. Box 718, Nadi, ph 72 988.

Jungle Cruise

A leisurely 2 hour river cruise on a 32 ft sheltered catamaran. The jovial tour guide "Humphry" will introduce you to a unique jungle area undisturbed by habitation and only accessible by boat. Afterwards visit the Regent of Fiji for a swim in the sea, or poolside snack. Free hotel pick-up and drop off. Bookings — South Sea Cruises, P.O. Box 718, Nadi Airport, ph 72 988.

All About Fiji in One Day
Combined morning jungle cruise up Nadi River and afternoon cruise aboard "Island Express". Coach pick-up from Nadi hotels from 8 am. At 11.30 am there is a poolside snack lunch at the Regent of Fiji, then off on a cruise to island resorts — Mana, Castaway, Club Naitasi and Plantation. Return sunset back to Regent of Fiji. For information — South Sea Cruises, P.O. Box 718, Nadi Airport, ph 72 988.

CORAL COAST

Hot Spring Tour
Departs Hideaway Resort at 10 am six days a week — weather permitting. Three hour tour through a tropical jungle to the hot springs and waterfall. Also involves a one hour walk along a creek. Bookings — Hideaway Resort, P.O. Box 233, Sigatoka, ph 50 177.

"Tui Tai" Fijian Hotel to Beachcomber Island
Departs the Fijian Hotel each Tuesday at 8 am. Sails along coral reefs, through Momi Passage to Beachcomber Island for lunch, then on to Lautoka where your coach returns you to the Fijian Hotel. For information — The Fijian Hotel Tour Desk, ph 50 155, or Islands In the Sun (Fiji) Ltd, P.O. Box 364, Lautoka, ph 61 500.

"Tui Tai" Vatulele Cruise
Full day cruise from the Coral Coast to the island of Vatulele, home of Fiji's legendary Red Prawns. Cruise departs Mondays at 9 am from Naviti Beach Resort and returns 5.15 pm. Coach transfers from all Coral Coast resorts and hotels. The Tui Tai is a 3-masted 140 ft schooner with a fully stocked bar on board. For reservations and further information — Islands In The Sun (Fiji) Ltd, P.O. Box 364, Lautoka, ph 61 500.

Coral Coast Railway
The restored "Fijian Princess" offers a 12 mile journey along the Coral Coast.
    The train travels along an historical sugarcane route through plantations, past coastal scenery and villages before arriving at

Natadola Beach. There are hostesses on board to ensure a comfortable trip. Included in the trip are fresh Fijian fruits on the outward journey, a BBQ lunch at the beach, and afternoon tea on the return journey.

The "Fijian Princess" departs the Yanuca Island Station (opposite the Fijian Hotel) at 9.45 am daily and returns to the station at approximately 5.30 pm. Seat reservations are recommended — Yanuca Island Station, P.O. Box 9755, Nadi Airport, ph 50 757 (8.30 am–5.30 pm).

SUVA

Wilderness Adventure Canoe Tour
Full day excursions for the adventurous. Pick up from Suva Hotels is at 9 am, then there is a 2 hour scenic tour of Viti Levu on the way to the upper reaches of the Navua River. If you have never canoed before then professional boatmen, who accompany the tour, provide instruction in the art of paddling. The highlight of the trip is a picnic lunch and swim amidst cascading waterfalls and a forest abounding in birdlife and exotic flora. Further information — Wilderness Adventures (Fiji) Ltd, P.O. Box 1389, Suva, ph 313 500.

Orchid Island Fijian Cultural Centre
Orchid Island is a natural formation in a river 10km from Suva on the Queens Road. A typical village, with a pre-European Fijian temple and chief's bure is located here. The temple was the first to have been built for over 100 years. There is an extensive collection of flora and fauna, handicraft demonstrations, and a good coverage of Fijian history, with a yaqona ceremony and traditional entertainment.

Buses leave Suva daily except Sundays between 9.35 am and 10.15 am, returning at 1.15 pm. You may visit at any time at your own convenience.

Explore the Interior
Full day tour. Capture the spirit of early Fiji by exploring the interior. Journey approximately 20 km up the Navua river, past villages, cascading waterfalls, deep gorges and the beauty of the tropical jungle. Stop at a Fijian village for swimming, with a traditional Fijian lunch served in the Meeting House. Coach/car departs daily from Suva and Pacific Harbour. Further information — Adventures Tours Ltd, P.O. Box 1389, Suva, ph 313 500.

Sigatoka Valley

Full day tour. Travel south from Suva along the main highway to Sigatoka town and the Sigatoka River. Drive along the river to the agricultural area known as Fiji's Salad Bowl. Return to town by the high level road. Then on to Tambua Sands, where lunch is available. Return to your hotel via the Queens Road. Departure time arranged when bookings confirmed. For information — Road Tours of Fiji Limited, P.O. Box 9268, Nadi Airport, ph 72 935.

Inland Safari and Island Tour

Minimum 8–12 day tour. Departs on a Sunday at 8.30 am. Hiking, horseriding, boating, visit to Fijian villages, river fish drives and Ovalau Island excursions. Further information — Mr. Naibose, P.O. Box 3014, Lami, ph 312 129.

Yanuca Island Picnic Cruise

Sail on the Longships — Pacific Harbour International Resort's twin-hulled catamaran. Departs Pacific Harbour marina at 10 am and returns at 4.30–5 pm — 5 days a week. BBQ lunch, snorkelling equipment, beach towels, village tour (except Sundays) included. Minimum of 6 persons. For enquiries and reservations — hotel activities desk, ph 45 011.

Coral See Cruise

Full and half day cruises aboard luxury glass bottom boat. Visit a tropical island with a palm fringed sandy beach. Complimentary morning tea and fresh luncheon. Departs daily from the Tradewinds Hotel at 9 am; city landing at 9.30 am. Half day cruise returns to Suva at 1 pm, full day cruise returns at 3.30 pm. For information — Tropic Cruises Fiji Ltd, P.O. Box 852, Suva, ph 386 319/381 570.

Rewa Delta-Nabua Village

Half day tour with a difference. Travels through farmlands to the Rewa River, then down the river by water taxi to Nailili Catholic Mission and St Joseph's Church. Continues along Nasali River to Nabua village where the ancient art of Fijian pottery making is demonstrated. There is an opportunity to view the village and meet the people, and then to call in at a small landing on the river to take a bush walk in the tropical jungle. Refreshments are served prior to crossing the river. The ancient art of mat weaving using voivoi leaves is also demonstrated. On the return drive to Suva, a visit is made to a Hindu temple. For information — Adventure Tours, P.O. Box 1389, Suva, ph 313 500.

RAKIRAKI

Sugar Mill Tour
Half day tour. Leaves the Rakiraki Hotel at 10 am and returns at 2 pm. Taxi or hotel transport available. For bookings — Rakiraki Hotel, P.O. Box 31, Rakiraki, ph 94 101.

Catholic Mission Tour
Half day tour. Leaves the Rakiraki Hotel at 8 am. Taxi or bus transport available. View the famous murals at Navunibitu Catholic Mission, portraying the Madonna and Christ in black. Bookings — Rakiraki Hotel, ph 94 101.

Nananu I-Ra Island Tour
Full day tour. Leaves Rakiraki Hotel at 9.30 am and returns at 4.30 pm. Lunch is included. Transportation provided. Bookings — Rakiraki Hotel, ph 94 101.

Vatukoula Gold Mine Tour
Afternoon and evening tour. Leaves Rakiraki Hotel at 2 pm and returns at 10 pm. Dinner and transportation included. Bookings — Rakiraki Hotel, ph 94 101.

OUTER ISLANDS

Vanua Levu — Savusavu

Buca Bay Tour
Full day tour. Leaves from Hot Springs Hotel at 9 am daily for a drive along the Hibiscus Highway to Buca Bay. Packed lunch is provided. Bookings — Hot Springs Hotel, P.O. Box 208, Savusavu, ph 86 ext. 181.

Copra Plantation Tour
Half day tour. Leaves from Hot Springs Hotel at 9 am and returns at noon. Bookings — Hot Springs Hotel, ph 86 ext. 181.

Batiri Citrus Orchard
Full day tour to the orange, pineapple, watermelon and passionfruit

plantation. Leaves from Hot Springs Hotel in the morning. Bookings — Hot Springs Hotel, ph 86 ext. 181.

Sail and Dive

Pacific Island Divers and Yacht Charters, based at Savu Savu offer extended dive charters to reefs in the Northern Island Group aboard a fully provisioned yacht. For information — Na Koro Resort, c/- P.O. Savusavu, ph 86 188 or after hours 86 179.

Tour to Labasa

This tour leaves the Hot Springs Hotel at 8.30 am each morning to drive via Savusavu town and Yaroi Village, then past the Copra Mill and around Savaudradra Bay before rising over the Delaikoro Hills. The road goes through Fijian farmlands and isolated villages, then areas that today are being rediscovered because of their gold bearing potential. Near the top of the rise there is a change in climate and with it a change of agricultural growth. Pine Plantation predominates. Prior to this is the turnoff to Nabouwalu, which is the closest point to Viti Levu, and the Satellite Town of Seaqaqa, on the main road before Labasa and the outer limits of the sugar cane area. At Labasa the cane crushing mill stands out, and beyond the mill there is an extra tour to the wood veneer factory at Malau. The return journey begins at 2.30 pm so as to arrive back at the hotel by 4.30 pm. Bookings — Hot Springs Hotel, ph 86 ext. 81.

A Day on the Bay

There is a day cruise beginning at 9.30 am from Savusavu, returning about 3.30 pm. The morning is spent sailing to the lower part of the bay with a stop for swimming and snorkelling before having lunch either on board or on the beach. After lunch cruise to Lesiaceva Point where another swimming/snorkelling stop can be arranged.

The afternoon cruise departs at 1.30 pm returning about 4.30 pm. A stop for afternoon snacks and drinks gives the visitors time for a swim off Lesiaceva Point.

Sunset cruise departs between 3 pm and 4 pm, depending on the season and the time of sunset, and returns about 6 pm or 7 pm. This is a leisurely sail around the Bay to see the spectacular sunset. For information — Emerald Yacht Charters Ltd, P.O. Box 225, Savusavu, ph 10.

Savusavu Copra Mill Tour
This tour leaves the Savusavu Hot Springs Hotel at 10 am in the morning and proceeds through Savusavu town to the east, and on past Yaroi Fijian Village. It then continues around the bottom of Savaudradra Bay to where the newly established Copra Oil Mill operates, about 5km away. There is a conducted tour through the Mill, and on the return journey there is an opportunity to stop off to visit the Savusavu market to see the wide variety of local produce. Bookings — Savusavu Hot Springs Hotel, ph 86 ext. 81.

Taveuni

Korolevu Island Coral Viewing
The tour departs from Castaway Gardens Resort daily, and a packed lunch is provided by the hotel on the island. Bookings — Castaway Gardens Resort, Box 1, Waiyevo, Taveuni, ph 87 ext. 286.

Waterfall Tour
This is also a daily tour from Castaway Gardens, visiting magnificent Bouma Waterfall. Lunch is not included. Bookings — Castaway Gardens Resort, ph 87 ext. 286.

Ovalau
Daily tours operate from Levuka to Rukuruku and return. Round Ovalau Safari tour can be arranged, and a day tour to Koroduadua Falls. Bookings — Tuni Tours, P.O. Box 112, Levuka, Ovalau, ph 43 329.

RECREATION

Swimming
Waters surrounding the Fiji Islands are warm year round. With the protection of barrier reefs, the waters off hotel and resort beaches are safe for swimming. Ocean temperatures average 25.5°C (78°F) in winter, and 27.7°C (82°F) in summer. The majority of hotels and resorts have fresh water swimming pools.

Scuba Diving
The reefs and lagoons of the Fiji Islands offer some of the finest diving in the world. Expert instruction, assistance and guides are available from the following companies:

Pacific Island Divers and Yacht Charter Ltd, based in Savusavu area.

Full PADI Certification and Resort Introductory courses for beginners. Daily dive charters — c/- P.O. Savusavu, ph 86 188.

Scubahire Ltd, operating from the Tradewinds Hotel Marina in Suva and Pacific Harbour International Resort in Deuba. Full and half day trips for scuba divers as well as snorkellers to local reefs. For information contact Pacific Harbour International Resort, G.P.O. Box 777, Suva, ph 361 088.

Aqua-Trek Ocean Sports Adventures is a fully accredited PADI training facility operating at Plantation Island Resort. Beginner and advanced diving courses. Also servicing Musket Cove and Club Naitasi — P.O. Box 9176, Nadi Airport, ph 72 333.

Dive Centre (Fiji) Ltd services Beachcomber and Treasure Islands. PADI Training facility with certification courses, introductory diving and night diving available. P.O. Box 3066, Lami, ph 314 599 (Suva) and 62 600 (Lautoka).

Sea Sports Ltd has daily dive charters from the Hyatt Regency, Fijian Resort and Naviti Beach Resort. PADI Certification and Introductory courses with 10 qualified instructors. P.O. Box 65, Korolevu, ph 50 598.

Dive Expeditions (Fiji) Ltd offer 5 night/6 day diving trips to the Yasawa Islands. Bure accommodation for divers at Yalovi Village on Waya Island. P.O. Box 502, Lautoka, ph 60 496.

Dive Taveuni specialises in dives on Rainbow Reef. The 11 m aluminium catamaran 'Lelewai II' takes divers to the reef. No hire gear available. Bookings — c/- P.O. Matei, Taveuni, ph 406M, Taveuni.

Mana Divers, at Mana Island Resort, off Lautoka. Two experienced dive masters take visiting divers to the reefs near the resort. Bookings — c/- Mana Island, P.O. Box 610, Lllautoka, ph 61 246.

Qamea Dive, located on Qamea Island off Taveuni. Daily dive trips are offered to nearby reefs. Two experienced dive guides on staff. P.O. Box Matei, Taveuni, ph Taveuni 220.

Matagi Island Dive operates from Matagi Island (6 miles off Taveuni), and offers full day boat diving excursion with unlimited diving or two dives a day. Equipment available for hire. P.O. Box 83, Waiyevo, Taveuni, ph 87 ext. 260.

Astrolabe Divers offer accommodation and diving packages on the island of Kadavu, about 150 km south of Viti Levu, in conjunction with Plantation Hideaway Resort. The accommodation is bure style at the Nuku Balovu Resort. For information contact Astrolabe Divers, c/- Plantation Hideaway Resort, Malau, P.O. Naleca, Kadavu, ph Naleca Post Office, 42 090, and leave message.

Sailing

Fiji has a full range of sailing craft to satisfy the enthusiast. Crafts are available for hire at most resorts.

Yacht Charters

Local or extended trips are available from:

La Violante, 103 ft (31.7 m) schooner. Stardust Cruises Ltd, Private Mail Bag, Nadi Airport, ph 62 215.

Whale's Tale, 100 ft (30 m) schooner. Ocean Schooner Co, P.O. Box 9625, Nadi Airport, ph 72 455.

Tau, 94 ft (29 m) schooner. Tradewinds Marine Ltd, P.O. Box 3084, Lami, Suva, ph 361 796.

Mollie Dean, 75 ft (23 m) power. Mollie Dean Cruises, P.O. Box 3256, Lami, Suva, ph 361 652.

Rainbow, 36 ft (11.2 m) ketch, and Kita, 35 ft (10.6 m) ketch. Emerald Yacht Charters, P.O. Box 15, Savusavu, ph 86 10.

Seax of Legra, 45 ft (13.8 m) ketch. Warwick and Dianne Bain, P.O. Box 89, Taveuni, Waiyevo. Telephone messages c/- Maravu; Taveuni 401A or marine R/T 3DN 6163.

Game Fishing

A variety of vessels are available for deepsea fishing charters:

Dau Wai, 25 ft (7.5 m) fast twin hull catamaran, based at The Regent of Fiji, ph 71 445.

Dau Siwa — 5 sports fishing boats, based at the Regent of Fiji, ph 761 445.

Fleet Lady, 43 ft (13.26 m) based at The Fijian Resort, ph 50 155.

Commander One, 42 ft vessel based in Suva, ph 361 128.

Serenawai, 27 ft based at The Hyatt Regency Fiji. Available every day except Sundays, on a two-hour basis, ph 50 555.

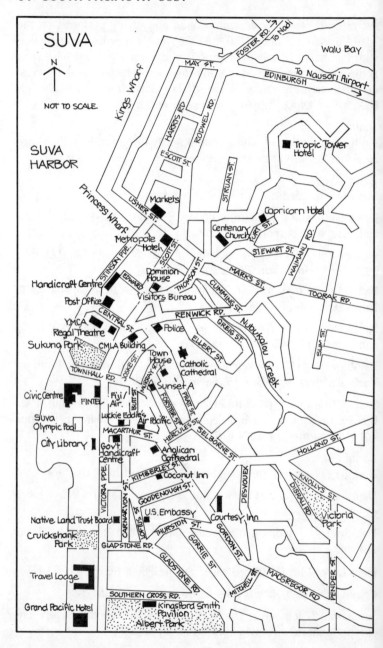

Sereki Mai, 48 ft De Fever motor cruiser powered by twin diesel engines, based at Navini Island Resort, ph 62 188.

MV Marau, 36 ft (12 m) based at Pacific Harbour and Toberua Island Resort. Available every day. Powered by twin diesel engines, has two fighting chairs and latest fishing equipment. A crew of two, ph 45 347 Pacific Harbour.

MV Marau II, 32 ft (10 m) based at Pacific Harbour International Hotel. Available every day. Powered by twin Volvo turbo charged diesel engines. Two fighting chairs, ph 45 347 Pacific Harbour.

Windsurfing
This a very popular sport in Fiji and most resorts cater for it. Equipment is available free of charge as part of the hotel facilities.

Surfing
There are only two locations in Fiji where the reefs provide breakers for surfing — Tavarua Island Surfing Base, P.O. Box 1419, Nadi, ph 50 309. Hideaway Resort, P.O. Box 233, Sigatoka, ph 50 177.

Tennis
Tennis is a growing sport in Fiji. Some of the best courts are located at hotels and resorts. The top facility is the John Newcombe Tennis Ranch at the Regent of Fiji. In Suva, Victoria Park has excellent courts, bookings, ph 313 428. Flood-lit courts are available for night games.

Golf
Considered the best in the South Pacific is the Pacific Harbour 18 hole championship course at Deuba, designed by Robert Trent Jones Jr. The only other 18 hole course is the Fiji Golf Club in Suva. Nine-hole courses can be found at Nadi, Lautoka, Ba, Rakiraki, Vatukoula, Nausori, Labasa, The Fijian Hotel, Naviti Resort, Reef Hotel and at Soqulu Plantation on the island of Taveuni.

Horse Riding
Many resorts in Fiji offer horse riding as part of their activities (one also offers donkey rides). Suva has a riding stable and a pony club.

Squash
There are squash courts in Suva at the following clubs: Fiji Club; Defence Club; United Club; Marist Club; Tamavua Club; and

Merchants Club.

There are also squash courts in Lautoka, Nadi, Levuka and at the Hyatt Regency Resort.

Jogging
Because of its ideal climate and lush landscape Fiji has proved a popular venue for joggers. Hash House Harriers and Harriets are local jogging clubs that hold events throughout the year.

Rugby
Rugby is Fiji's major national sport. It is played in the cooler months from April to September. Fiji National teams have toured such countries as the British Isles, France, USA, Canada, Hong Kong and of course the neighbouring countries of Australia and New Zealand. The Fijians are famous for their natural flare, running with the ball — win or lose it doesn't seem to matter.

Soccer
Soccer is played between March and October. Major tournaments during this period are the National League, the Battle of the Giants and the greatest event of the year — the Interdistrict Tournament, played during the Independence weekend in October.

Cricket
Played from mid-October to Easter. Main centres for cricket are Lautoka, Suva and Nadi, but it is also played in the outer islands of Lakeba, Vanuabalavu, Ovalau, Ono-I-Lau and Taveuni. A number of cricket teams from overseas have visited Fiji and played against local groups. The Fiji National Team has toured New Zealand, Australia, Papua New Guinea and the United Kingdom. Visiting teams are always welcome.

Lawn Bowls
The Suva Bowling Club, along the capital's waterfront, has two international size, floodlit greens. Visitors are welcome to use the club's facilities. Also standard size greens can be found at The Fijian Resort, The Regent of Fiji, Rakiraki Hotel, Lautoka City, Levuka town in Ovalau and at Vatukoula.

Part of downtown Suva, Fiji

Beachcomber Island, Fiji

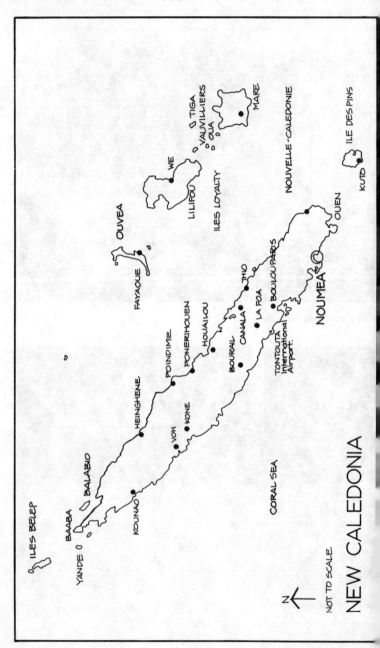

NEW CALEDONIA

NOT TO SCALE

NEW CALEDONIA

New Caledonia has a surface area of about 19,000 km² (7,334 sq miles), situated between 18S and 22S, 163E and 168E. The main island has an elongated shape about 50 km (31 miles) wide and 400 km (248 miles) long. It is surrounded by more than 800 km (496 miles) of barrier reef enclosing one of the most beautiful lagoons in the world. New Caledonia includes the following:

— The Mainland.
— Ouen Island and the Isle of Pines to the south.
— The Loyalty Islands (Mare, Lifou, Ouvea, Beautemps-Beaupre and Tiga) to the east.
— The Belep, Surprise and Chesterfield Islands to the north.

A central chain of mountains extends the length of the mainland, the highest peaks rising to between 1,200 and 1,600 m (3,924 and 5,232 ft). This mountainous backbone creates a natural division into two distinct regions:

The east coast is narrow, with night rainfall and fresh trade winds. This coastline has varied tropical vegetation including large coconut plantations at the foot of waterfalls or enclosed in valleys through which rivers pass on their way to the sea. The west coast, in the leeward side of the island, is broad and ideally suited to cattle farming and agriculture. Covered mostly by gum-tree savannah, the west coast offers many interesting areas for the tourist.

HISTORY

On September 4, 1774, Captain James Cook discovered these islands which he called New Caledonia because the mountains in the Balade area — where he anchored — reminded him of Scotland (in Latin: Caledonia).

The country was inhabited by Melanesians, later called Canaques, a term derived from Polynesian language meaning "man". After a short stay at Balade, Cook sailed his vessel, the "Resolution", to Amere Island near the Isle of Pines, without catching sight of the Loyalty Islands. In 1792 the Frenchman Bruni d'Entrecasteaux, while

59

searching for the missing navigator Laperouse, also made a stop at Balade and the Isle of Pines. And it was at Balade that the first Catholic missionaries landed in 1843. They had been preceded by Protestant missionaries in the Loyalty Islands, which had finally been discovered. Once more at Balade, on September 24, 1853, by order of Napoleon III, Admiral Febvrier-Despointes officially took possession of New Caledonia.

In 1862, Admiral Guillain became the first governor. Two years later New Caledonia was established as a penal settlement receiving thousands of convicts and political prisoners (in particular those from the uprising of the Paris Commune between 1872 and 1878). With the arrival of Governor Feillet free colonisation grew and from 1897 the transportation of convicts ceased.

New Caledonia developed slowly, not without difficulties, up to the outbreak of World War II. In 1940, it was one of the first French colonies to join General de Gaulle's Free France. From 1942–45 the territory became an important American military base, an exposure that led the country into modern-day development.

New Caledonia is a part of the Republic of France. Its people are consequently French citizens and participate in the presidential elections as well as electing two deputies and a senator to the French Parliament.

The Territory is composed of four regions: The Eastern, The Western, The Southern and The Loyalty Islands.

The High Commissioner is the State official in New Caledonia, and is responsible for the legality of the actions of the local regional or territorial authorities.

CLIMATE

Cooled by the surrounding Pacific Ocean and refreshing tradewinds, New Caledonia enjoys a sunny climate marked by two seasons: December to March, warm and humid with moderate rainfall; April to November cool and dry. The climate is comparable with spring weather.

POPULATION

The total population is approximately 144,000 of whom 61,000 are Melanesians, 54,000 Europeans, 17,000 Wallisians and Tahitians, 12,000 Indonesians and Vietnamese. The average population density is 7 per sq km.

LANGUAGE

Although there are numerous native dialects, French is the common language of New Caledonia. English is understood in the hotels and resorts, and is taught in the schools, but the people in the streets and shops of Noumea either can't or won't answer your English questions.

PUBLIC HOLIDAYS

January 1	New Year's Day
March/April	Good Friday/Easter Monday
May 1	Labour Day
May 12	Ascension Day
May 23	Whitday
July 14	National/Bastille Day
August 15	Assumption Day
September 24	New Caledonia Day
November 1	All Saints Day
November 11	Armistice Day
December 25	Christmas

A Noumea resort, New Caledonia

ENTRY REGULATIONS

A valid passport and an onward or return ticket are required. A visa is also required for all except French citizens and people from EEC countries. Smallpox vaccination certificates are not required for passengers arriving direct from Australia, New Zealand, USA, Canada or EEC countries.

In addition to personal effects, the duty free allowance is 200 cigarettes or 50 cigars or 8 ounces of tobacco plus 1 litre of spirts. For the amateur photographer a stay of less than 30 days allows several cameras to be imported duty free.

EMBASSIES

Australia:	19–21 avenue du Marechal Foch, Noumea, ph 272 414.
New Zealand:	4 Boulevard Vauban, Noumea, ph 272 543.
UK:	No resident representative. Refer to High Commission in Canberra, Australia, ph 61 (62) 73 0422.
US:	No resident representative. Refer to Embassy in Wellington, NZ, ph 64 (4) 722 068.
Canada:	No resident representative. Refer to High Commission in Canberra, Australia, ph 61 (62) 73 3844.

MONEY

The monetary unit of New Caledonia is the French Pacific Franc (CFP). Approximate exchange rates are:

A$	=	CFP94.00
NZ$	=	72.00
US$	=	115.00
UK£	=	196.00
Can$	=	97.00

COMMUNICATIONS

The General Post Office is near the museum on rue Eugene Porcheron, Noumea, ph 274 881. Opening hours are 7.15–11.15 am and 1.30–5.30 pm. Stamps are sold at main hotels, stationers and supermarkets. There are telephone, telex and cable services throughout the mainland, plus ISD phones over all of New Caledonia. The country code is 687.

There are 7 local radio stations (4 in Noumea, 3 inland). Five of them broadcast between 6 am and 10 pm, and the other two 24 hours a day. There are two TV channels transmitting local, metropolitan and international programmes in colour.

There is one daily newspaper Les Nouvelles Caledoniennes and two weekly, Tele 7 Jours and Les Nouvelles HEBDO.

MISCELLANEOUS
Local time is GMT + 11 hours.

Business Hours
Banks: 7.30 am–3.45 pm Monday to Friday.
Shops and Offices: 7.30–11.30 am and 2–6 pm. Most close at lunch
  time.

Electricity supply is 220 volts AC., 50 cycles (two-prong plugs).

There is no departure tax.

Credit cards are widely accepted.

No Tipping.

Hotel Tax — depending on the classification of the hotel 140 CFP, 280 CFP or 380 CFP is to be paid per room-night.

Emergencies — dial 17.

Medical Facilities
Doctor, dentist, hospital, clinic, pharmacy and urgent dispensary facilities are available.

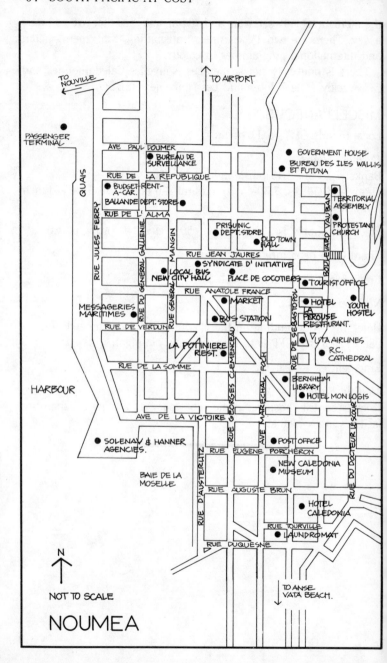

NOUMEA

A Polynesian lass

Accommodation at Bora Bora

Blow-holes of Tongatapu, Tonga

TRAVEL INFORMATION

HOW TO GET THERE

By Air

Tontouta International Airport, Noumea, is served by five international airlines: UTA French Airlines, Qantas, Air New Zealand, Air Nauru and Air Caledonie International.

Weekly flights: San Francisco and Los Angeles via Papeete (2), Paris via Singapore and Jakarta (2), Sydney (6), Brisbane (1), Melbourne (1), Nadi (1), Auckland (3), Port Vila (5), Naura (2) and Tokyo (1).

Transport from the airport to the city is by Tourist coach (CFP1,300/1,500), Blue bus (CFP320) or car (CFP4,500/5,000).

By Sea

Noumea is an international port served by the following shipping lines: Chandris, CTC, P & O, Princess Cruises and Sitmar, Polish Ocean Lines.

TOURIST INFORMATION

The Office Territorial du Tourisme, 25 Avenue Marechal Foch, Noumea, ph 272 632.

ACCOMMODATION

Accommodation in New Caledonia is rated under the 1-star, 2-star, etc. system, with the more stars the better, and more expensive.
The prices listed here are for a double room per night, and are in French Pacific Francs.

Noumea

3-star

Escapade Resort, Ilot Maitre Island, ph 285 320 — CFP9,200; Isle De France — Apartments, Anse Vata, ph 262 422 — CFP10,000; Noumea Beach, Baie des Citrons, ph 262 055 — CFP9,200; Nouvata Beach, Anse Vata, ph 282 200 — CFP8,900; Surf Novotel, Anse Vata, ph 286 688 — CFP10,500; Toutouel RC, Tontouta International Airport — CFP7,380

2-star

Club Mediterranee, Anse Vata Beach, ph 261 200 — CFP74,592 (per week); Hotel Ibis Noumea, Baie des Citrons, ph 285 320 — CFP9,800; Le Lagon, Anse Vata, ph 281 255 — CFP8,000; Lantana Beach, Anse Vata, ph 262 212 — CFP8,900; Mocambo, Baie des Citrons, ph 262 701 — CFP7,500; Motel Anse Vata, Anse Vata, ph 262 612 — CFP4,000; Noumea Village, City, ph 283 006 — CFP5,300; Paradise Park Motel, City suburb (Vallee des Colons) ph 272 541 — CFP6,900; Le Paris, City, ph 281 700 — CFP5,200;

1-star

Caledonia, City (Latin Quarter), ph 273 821 — CFP2,400; Laperouse, City, ph 272 251 — CFP4,880; Motel Le Bambou, Val Plaisance, ph 261 290 — CFP3,250; Trianon Hotel, city suburb, ph 262 492 — CFP3,000

There is a Youth Hostel in the city with 60 beds — ph 275 879.

West Coast

3-star

Evasion 130 RC, Sarramea, ph 421 235 — CFP4,000

2-star

Les Paillotes de le Ouenghi — RC, Boulouparis, ph 351 735 — CFP4,500.

1-star

Copellia, Koumac, ph 356 266 — CFP3,000; Hotel Douyere — RE, Bourall, ph 441 150 — CFP3,600

Not rated

Le Grand Cerf, Koumac, ph 356 131 — CFP3,500; Hotel Banu, La Foa, ph 421 119 — CFP2,800.

East Coast

2-star

Hotel de la Plage, Poindimie, ph 427 128 — CFP3,200.

1-star

Relais Alison - RE, Toubo, ph 428 812 — CFP3,500

Not rated

Tapoundari, Poindimie, ph 427 111 — CFP3,900.

South

3-star
La Siesta - RC, Plum, ph 433 577 — CFP3,500

Not rated
Vallon Dore, Monte-Dore, ph 433 208 — CFP3,500.

Camping
Most of the villages in the interior and on the islands have public camping facilities. Camping can also be arranged on tribal lodging properties.

LOCAL TRANSPORT

Bus
Mini-buses cover the whole city of Noumea and operate from the terminal near the baie de la Moselle. All bus fares are the same price, CFP90 within Noumea area.

Taxi
Taxis are to be found in the central square of Noumea, or contact Association des Radios Taxis de Noumea, ph 285 370.

Car
Car rental companies offer reasonable self-drive rates throughout the main island. Drive on the right and give way to the right. A current driver's licence is required — international not required.

Some names and numbers — Avis, ph 275 484; AB Location, ph 281 232; Europcar, ph 262 444; Hertz, ph 261 822; Mencar, ph 276 125; Noumea Car, ph 272 591.

Air
The domestic airline, Air Caledonie, flies daily from the local Magena Airport in Noumea to the Isle of Pines, Mare, Lifou and Ouvea, as well as regular flights to Touho (East Coast) and to Belep and Koumac (West Coast).

Air charters are available from: Air Caledonie, ph 252 177; Aviazur, ph 253 709, Helicocean, ph 253 949.

Sea
Cruises and charter boats have been included under Sightseeing. For Taxi Boats, try Esquinade Plaisance, ph 272 505.

EATING OUT

Eating out in New Caledonia ranges from the very best French provincial to the absolutely exotic. Chose from any of the national restaurants scattered throughout the city ... eat Chinese dishes cooked in true Cantonese or Mandarin style. Maybe you'd prefer authentic Indonesian, Tahitian or Vietnamese cuisine? They are all there. You can choose from expensive, medium or inexpensive — according to your budget or mood.

For lunch, try taking a casse-croute to the beach: a loaf of French bread, fruit and wine. Very cheap, very a la francaise.

The usual restaurant meal times are 11.30 am–2 pm and 7–11 pm. Most are open Sundays.

The Tourist Office has an excellent booklet entitled Bon Appetit, which tells of all the eating places in Noumea, with addresses, phone numbers, and even menus and prices. The booklet lists 55 places for snacks and 76 restaurants, so it is invaluable.

Noumea's night clubs are small and lively. Some stage the typical floorshow you would normally see on the Continent. Others feature exciting and colourful Polynesian spectaculars — the famous Tamure for one, provocative, sensual and typical of the Pacific. The clubs are dotted throughout the city, and on the two main beaches, Anse Vata and Baie des Citrons.

Casino (Anse Vata) is open every day from 4 pm–2 am. Try your luck at Black Jack, Baccarat, Roulette, Chemin de Fer, etc, but do not forget your passport. Jacket and tie are not compulsory, but a reasonable standard of dress is expected. Free gambling tokens (CFP1,000) are available at your hotel desk.

SHOPPING

Look for the red, white and blue "Duty-Free Shop" sign and shop for French perfume, cosmetics, scarves, shoes, hand-bags and jewellery at 20% to 30% discount prices. There is also a wide range of electrical goods, radios, cameras, watches, etc.

Usual souvenirs of this area are wooden sculptures influenced by Melanesian art, carved mother-of-pearl, gifts made of pandanus bark, shells, tapas (hand-painted bark cloth) and all manner of stones illustrating the geological wealth of the territory.

You have to be up early to catch the local market near the Place des Cocotiers, but it's worth the effort, and not just for the fresh fish, vegetables and tropical fruits. Big Wallisian or Tahitian women with their flower leis, Vietnamese wih black lacquered teeth and Indonesians wrapped in their sarongs provide a picturesque aspect of the country. The market is open every day from 5–10 am.

SIGHTSEEING

There are numerous half-day, full day and longer tours available from local tour operators and coach companies. For full details we suggest you contact one of the following.

Coach Companies
Arc En Ciel, P.O. Box 1244, ph 271 980; Aviabus, P.O. Box 183, Tontouta, ph 351 187; Golden Star, P.O. Box 624, ph 262 355; Pacific Holidays, P.O. Box 1524, ph 273 258; Scea, P.O. Box A3, Cedex, ph 286 100; Sitourcal, Imm. Center Foch, ph 278 140; Pourouoro, 27 bis Avenue du Marechal Foch, ph 282 842; Sunrise Tours, P.O. Box 4719, ph 281 869; T.T.T., P.O. Box 4853, ph 282 774.

Tour Operators
AMAC Tours, 31 Promenade Roger Laroque, ph 263 838; Center Voyages, 27 bis avenue du Marechal Foch, ph 284 040; Discovery Tours, 31 Promenade Roger Laroque, ph 263 131; Hibiscus Tours, P.O. Box 4853, ph 282 774; Orima, 27 bis avenue du Marechal Foch, ph 282 842; Pacific Holidays, 27 bis avenue du Marechal Foch, ph 273 258; South Pacific Tours, Shopping Center Vata, ph 262 320; S.S.E.A. (Shipping and Shore Excursions Agency) avenue James Cook, SATO Building, ph 281 122; Tours 33, 2 bis rue Charles de Verneith, Quartier Latin, ph 281 415.

Sea Cruises and Charter Boats
Amedee Lighthouse Excursion:
Samara, P.O. Box 3341, ph 262 312, "Mary D" and "Mary D-Hydroflite", P.O. Box 233, ph 263 131, Lady Diana, P.O. Box 2295, ph 261 248.

Diving Tours:
Nauticus, 59 avenue du Marechal Foch, ph 275 141.

Sailing Yacht Charters or Rental:
Noumea Yacht Charters, P.O. Box 1068, ph 286 666; Vagabund, P.O. Box 2883, ph 261 493; Captain Ad Hoc Cruises, P.O. Box 3621, ph 263 072; Alize-voiles, P.O. Box 4778, ph 275 043.

Glass Bottom Tours:
"Captain Cook", P.O. Box 2295, ph 261 248.

Charter Boats:
"Colleen", P.O. Box 4555, ph 262 829; "Ingrid Giovanni", P.O. Box 1654, ph 252 922; "Hoki Mai", P.O. Box 3982, ph 282 988; "Annabel et Patonga", c/- Mr. Viratells, Nouville.

Comfort Cruises:
"California" South Pacific Cruises, P.O. Box 233, ph 263 131.

Noumea

MAINLAND

Noumea City

Noumea was chosen as a port and the capital of New Caledonia in 1854. At first it was called Port de France but was changed to Noumea in 1866. The city is situated on a peninsula and has numerous coves and bays, some of them deep enough for anchorage. The most beautiful beaches are those of Anse Vata, Baie des Citrons and Magenta. At the centre of the city is the Place des Cocotiers shaded by Flame Trees, whose flowers are a sight at the end of the year. Surrounding the Place des Cocotiers are numerous streets full of shops. The city has a population of 60,000.

Aquarium

Located along Anse Vata, this aquarium is famous for its unique display of living corals and tropical sea-life.

Botanical Garden and Zoo

The Parc Forestier Michael Corbasson is 4 km from the centre of Noumea in the hilly area south of Montravel. It features typical flora and fauna and the unique New Caledonian Cagou bird.

Museum

This building, opened in 1971, displays the history and way of life of Melanesian people from Vanuatu, the Loyalty Islands and New Caledonia, as well as exhibiting typical flora and fauna. The museum is located in Baie de la Moselle, near the Post Office.

The South

In the south there are arid plains covered with endemic plants that cling to the rocks. A dense forest is found along the central mountain chain, where orchids and tree ferns flourish. Worth seeing are the dam at Yate, the Giant of Goro, the Madeleine and Wadiana waterfalls, and the lovely beach at Kuebini.

The North

From Poum to Balade, passing through Ouegoa, the north presents a beautiful vegetation and magnificent beaches of white sand. Mining in the Paagoumene/Poum area has been very important in the past. Worth seeing are the green valley of the Diahot, the longest river in New Caledonia, and Balade, on the East Coast, one of the main historical sites in the Territory.

The West Coast

The west coast is characterised by a gum-tree savannah, and large cattle stations interrupted here and there by mines. The villages are found in valleys inland from the coast, which has few good beaches because of the invasion of mangrove swamps.

Worth seeing are the Pierced Rock and Turtle bay, both 8 km from Bourail, and the Adio grottoes at Poya and Koumac.

The East Coast

The East Coast is the tourist haven, with tropical vegetation, beautiful beaches, numerous waterfalls and deeply enclosed valleys. Don't miss the strange rock formations at Hienghene — Les Tours de Notre-Dame, also called Poule couveuse (Broody Hen) which reach a height of 60m, and the beaches at Poindimie and Touho. Travelling towards Houailou, and further south, the mining country reminds one of the main wealth of the territory.

OUEN ISLAND

Separated from the main island by Woodin Strait, halfway between the mainland and the Isle of Pines, is the mountainous and barren Isle Ouen, well-known for its thousands of turtles and jade mines. The island's population is concentrated in the native village of Ouara, which can be reached by a graded road.

ISLE OF PINES

Jewel of the Pacific, this island is called Kounie by its inhabitants. It lies 70 km (43 miles) off the south-east of the mainland, and was discovered and named by Captain Cook in 1774. One hundred years ago, a convict settlement was established but seven years later the prisoners were removed to the mainland. The ruins of the prison colony and the Commune cemetery are still evident. The caves are worth a visit.

The unique pine trees which give the island its name sometimes reach 60 m in height. There are also sandalwood and rosewood trees, and the lagoon shelters turtles, lobsters and squillfish.

The village of Vao is the seat of the local council and the Chefferie built in traditional Melanesian style. During the months of March and April, the feast of the yams is one of the local events which must not be missed.

THE LOYALTY ISLANDS

This group of upraised coral atolls consists of the islands of Ouvea, Mare, Lifou and Tiga. Not only are there deserted beaches of golden sand, facing an azure and emerald sea, there are also grottoes and caves, and thousands of coconut palms shading thickets of hibiscus.

The archipelago of the Loyalty Islands is 100 km (62 miles) from the East Coast of mainland New Caledonia. There are about 50 km (31 miles) between each island, and their vegetation consists mainly of coconut and sandalwood trees.

Mare

The island has an area of 650 km^2 (251 sq miles) and a population of 4,400. On the west coast, Tadine is the most important town and the port. Marvellous scenery and beaches are to be found at Tawainedre, Penaloi Medu and Netche.

Ouvea

The smallest of the three main islands, Ouvea has an area of 130 km^2 (50 sq miles), and a population of 2,950. It is long and narrow with white sandy beaches bordered by coconut palms, and a lagoon abounding in sea life.

Fayaoue, surrounded by many native villages, is the administrative centre of the island. There is beautiful scenery on the road from Fayaoue to Saint-Joseph, and most of the islands of the north can be seen: Isle of the Whale, Isle of the Turtles, Isle of Pines and Ounes Island. The bay of Lekin and Mouli Island are worth a visit.

Lifou

The largest of the Loyalty Islands, Lifou has an area of 1,150 km^2 (444 sq miles) and 8,600 inhabitants. We, situated in the bay of Chateaubriand, is the main town and the administrative centre of the Loyalty Islands. Other villages include Chepenehe with interesting caves, Dueulu, Doking, Mou (renowned for the beauty of its beaches) and Nahalo.

Don't miss the Grande Case (Chief's Hut) and the beautifully decorated church.

Tiga

Tiga is a tiny island with luxuriant vegetation. It is approximately 6 km long and 2 km wide. The native village situated in the north has 150 people. The main resource of the island is copra.

RECREATION

For spectators and participants alike, special sporting events are held annually — Triathlon du Soleil in April, the International Tennis Week in September, the Sydney/Noumea Yacht Race (every second year), windsurfing championships in December, and many more. Check with the New Caledonia Tourist Office for details.

Le Cricket is a sport which is quite unique to New Caledonia in that up to three batspeople stand at each crease with bats high in the air, there are no overs, and the bowler and wicketkeeper swap roles as the need arises. The Melanesian women play most weekends in Noumea and the villages. The French game of petanque is played in the main square and at Anse Vata.

Because of the lagoon, water sports abound. Windsurfing, sailing, scuba diving, jet skiing, paddling a canoe and, of course, there are lots of beaches for swimming and snorkelling.

Golf — Dumbea Golf Club, 15 minutes from Noumea, ph 368 181.
Bowling — Le Commodore, Anse Vata, ph 262 602.
Squash — Squash Club, P.O. Box 2377, Noumea, ph 262 212.
Swimming Pool, Ouen Toro, ph 261 843.
Tennis — ph 264 532 for details.
Nature Safari 4WD — Pacific Raids, ph 252 086/282 325.
Aquatic Games Rental — Baie des Citrons beach and Amedee islet.

Also available are horse riding and clay shooting, and bicycles and mopeds can be rented. For more information on these contact the Tourist Information Office, ph 272 632.

Public swimming pools and tennis courts are available in some villages in the interior.

COMMENT

Fortunately the resorts of New Caledonia are self-sufficient, so there's really no need to ever leave them. The township of Noumea is not really very inviting, and everything is very expensive. Of course go and have a look-see, but don't allow too much of your holiday time for sightseeing there, as you will be very disappointed.

Typical South Pacific scene

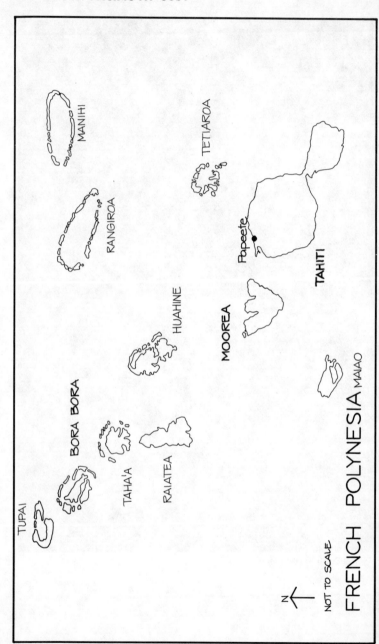

FRENCH POLYNESIA

Tahiti, the biggest island in French Polynesia, lies in the South Pacific, half-way between Australia and California, and approximately half-way between Tokyo and Santiago, at latitude 17S and longitude 151W.

French Polynesia covers an ocean area about the size of Europe (without Russia), but the total land area of the islands adds up to only 1,041 km² (1,544 sq miles). There are some 130 islands in five archipelagoes: the Society Islands (including Tahiti), Marquesas, Tuatomu archipelago, Gambiers and Australs. All these islands are of either volcanic or coral origin. Tahiti covers an area of 402 sq miles, and is dominated by the peaks of Orohena (2,244 m — 7,337 ft) and Aorai (2,075 m — 6,786 ft). Most of the islands of French Polynesia, even those of volcanic composition, are ringed by coral reefs.

HISTORY

French Polynesia extends over such a large area that it took several explorers and many years to discover and chart all the islands. The Spanish and the Dutch were first, making voyages through some archipelagoes during the 16th and 17th centuries. The first European to discover Tahiti was the English Captain Samuel Wallis in HMS Dolphin in 1767. Frenchman Louis de Bougainville followed in 1768 and Captain James Cook in 1769. In 1788 Captain William Bligh arrived in HMS Bounty to collect breadfruit trees. It was here that the famous Mutiny occurred, when Fletcher Christian seized the ship and put Bligh to sea in a small open boat. Bligh sailed that boat and seventeen men across three thousand miles of the Pacific to Indonesia, and lived to see most of the mutineers caught and brought to justice. Fletcher Christian escaped the noose, only to die a violent death at the hands of Tahitians in a dispute over women and land on tiny Pitcairn Island.

It first seemed to these Europeans, and their crews, that they had discovered the lost Eden. Not only were the islands extraordinarily beautiful, they seem to provide the natives with all they needed for a comfortable life. Breadfruit trees and other food plants grew in abundance, and only needed gathering, the lagoons were well-stocked with fish and shellfish, and the ocean beyond the reef had great schools of tuna. The climate was such that the people managed with few clothes and very simple houses without walls to allow the cooling breezes to flow through.

In reality the natives lived in a rigidly structured society with the majority no better than slaves, and thieving was rife. The climate was indeed idyllic, but bred the mosquito which carried filariasis, a parasite which when injected into the bloodstream multiplies with horrifying results to the human body. The people were also prone to large disfiguring ulcers, which were in later years diagnosed as yaws, a bacterial skin disease. Cures for both these diseases were not discovered until nearly 200 hundred years later.

There were constant wars between the different tribes, with the victors making slaves of the conquered, taking over their land, and bringing back as trophies the heads of men, women and children.

Even so the Tahitians would probably have been better off without the "invasion" of the Europeans who brought with them not only civilisation, but venereal disease, alcohol and measles, to which the natives had no immunity. Papeete became a centre of much boozing and brawling until the French took possession in the 1840s.

The islands may have lost much of their native population, but the Eden reputation lasted, and many famous people have lived there and written romantic tales or painted the magnificent scenery — people such as Robert Louis Stevenson, Herman Melville, Charles Darwin, Pierre Loti (Julian Viaud), Jack London, Somerset Maugham, Rupert Brooke, Paul Gauguin and James A. Michener.

In 1957, French Polynesia became a French Overseas Terriory. As such, it is headed by a High Commissioner representing the French Republic. The legislative body is the Territorial Assembly, consisting of 30 members elected by popular vote; it elects the 7 councillors who compose the Government Council. French Polynesia also elects representatives to the French Senate, Parliament and Economic and Social Council.

CLIMATE

Cooled by the gentle breezes of the Pacific, the climate of these islands is sunny and pleasant. Roughly speaking there are two seasons: from December to February the climate is warm and moist

(22°C-32°C,72°F-90°F); from March through November the climate is cool and dry (17°C-22°C, 64F°-72°F). Most of the rain falls during the warm season.

POPULATION

French Polynesia has a population of more than 167,000, with more than half living in Tahiti. Papeete, the capital of the Territory has a population of 24,000 Polynesians of which the Maori race accounts for 75%, Asians 10% and Europeans 15%.

Many religions are represented, including Roman Catholic, Protestant, Mormon, Seventh Day Adventist, the Reorganised Church of Jesus Christ of the Latter Day Saints, Jehovah Witness, Judaism and Buddhism.

LANGUAGE

The official languages are French and Tahitian, but almost everyone serving tourists speaks English.

PUBLIC HOLIDAYS AND FESTIVALS

Several of the events listed on this calendar do not have definite dates and are subject to modification within the first few months of the year. For further information please contact OPAC, the Territorial Cultural Center, P.O. Box 1709, Papeete, Tahiti, ph (689) 42 88 50.

January 1	New Year's Day — a public holiday in all the Islands.
February–March	Chinese New Year.
March 5	Missionaries Day — this is Tahiti's own special holiday, commemorating the arrival of the Protestant missionaries from the London Missionary Society on March 5, 1797, at Matavai Bay.
April–May	During these two months many beauty queens are chosen, to represent sports clubs, philanthropic associations, the Chinese community and other groups.
May	Taupiti O Papeete. Miss Papeete is elected and a carnival atmosphere reigns, with rides, games and contests, with the important activities taking place on the weekends. These preliminary festivities are

	a build-up for the Papeete Centennial celebration in 1990.
May	Second Pacific Festival of Underwater Images. A contest is open to the public to contribute colour slides and photos of the underwater life in the islands of Tahiti and other marine locales. These images are exhibited at OTAC, the Territorial Cultural Center.
June	Annual Moorea International Triathlon. An endurance test in which participants must swim 2 km, cycle 60 km and run 15 km.
June 5	World Environment Day — An all-day programme at Point Venus includes exhibits, films, skits, song and dance performances.
June	Election of Miss Tahiti and Miss Heiva.
June–July	Marquesas Festival of Arts "Te Mata Vaa O Te Henua Enana" takes place in Taiohae, Nuku Hiva. Traditional Marquesan songs, chants and dances, preparation of popoi and other culinary exhibits, tapa making, carving sculptures and tattooing are featured.
July	Heiva I Tahiti. This is the most important festival of the year, when people come from all around the world to film and photograph the colourful events and to join in the fun. Highlights include songs and dance competitions, outrigger canoe races, contests of copra preparation, stone lifting, basket and hat weaving. There are permanent exhibits in the Arts and Crafts Village, traditional costume making, fire walking ceremonies, historic re-enactments at Marae Arahurahu and other religious and cultural exhibits and events. The festival may begin on June 30 and continue through to July 23.
July 14	Bastille Day. France's National Holiday is celebrated in Papeete with a big parade, parties and an all-night ball.
July	Annual Tahiti International Pro-Am Open. Generally played at the Olivier Breaud Inter-

	national Golf Course at Atimaono. The Tahiti Open is played toward the end of July.
August	International Marathon of Tahiti-Moorea. A 40 km race with $15,000 in prizes, begins at Vaiare on Moorea, and a semi-marathon race of 20 km with $5,000 in prizes starts in Haapiti.
September 8	Anniversary of the Statute of Internal Autonomy of French Polynesia.
October 6	Day of the Tree. This is a week long event, with environmental and folkloric activities.
October	Stone Fishing Ceremony in Tahaa "Heiva No Te Pahu Nui O Tahaa". This two-day event includes boat races, a fire walking ceremony and a fun-filled day on a "motu" islet in the Tahaa Lagoon.
November 1	All Saints Day. Flower stands are set up all around the island of Tahiti, with families spending the day decorating the graves in all the cemeteries in Papeete, Faaa, Arue and Punaauia.
December 2	Tiare Tahiti Day. Tahiti's national flower, the fragrant white "Gardenia Taitensis" is honored, with a Tiare Tahiti being presented to everyone on the streets of Papeete, in the hotels and at the airport.
December 24–25	Christmas. This is summertime in the islands of Tahiti, and all the flowers are in bloom. Santa Claus or Pere Noel, makes his appearance several times, and hotels and restaurants present special menus and entertainment for these two days.
December 31	New Year's Eve. Hotels and restaurants in Tahiti and the other islands go all out to make sure the ritual of St. Sylvester is properly enjoyed.

ENTRY REGULATIONS

A valid passport is required, and a visa is required by all except nationals of EEC countries.

Vaccinations are not necessary unless visitors are from an infected area.

In addition to personal effects, 200 cigarettes or 50 cigars or 250gm of tobacco and 2 litres of spirits are allowed duty free.

Please note: All passengers embarking from Fiji and Pago Pago must have their baggage, except hand luggage, fumigated upon arrival in Tahiti. Since fumigation takes about 2 hours, passengers should carry clothing and toilet articles for a night's stay in Tahiti in their hand luggage. Baggage undergoing fumigation can be left at the airport in bond and picked up later the same or the following day by hotels, tour operators or guides on behalf of the passengers. While all this may cause minor inconvenience, it is necessary to protect Tahiti's coconut trees against pests found on some islands of the South Pacific.

EMBASSIES

Australia: No resident representative. Refer to High Commission in Wellington, NZ, ph 64 (4) 637 411.

New Zealand: c/- Air New Zealand, Ltd, Papeete, ph 430 170.

US: No resident representative. Refer to US Embassy in Wellington, NZ, ph 64 (4) 722 068.

UK: No resident representative. Refer to High Commission in Wellington, NZ, ph 64 (4) 726 049.

Canada: No resident representative. Refer to High Commission in Wellington, NZ, ph 64 (4) 637 411.

MONEY

The currency used in Tahiti and French Polynesia is the French Pacific Franc (FCFP). Notes are in demonations of 5,000, 1,000 and 500 Francs CFP. Coins are in denominations of 100, 50, 25, 10, 5, 2 and 1 Franc CFP.

Approximate rates of exchange, which should be used only as a guide, are:

A$	=	CFP94.00
NZ$	=	72.00
US$	=	115.00
UK£	=	196.00
Can$	=	97.00

COMMUNICATIONS

Mail, telephone, telegrams and telex services are available. In Papeete, the Post Office is the center of international communications. Here stamps may be purchased, and cables may be sent through Telefrance during postal hours. International and local inter-island calls may also be placed at hotels. IDD service is available and the country code is 689. All calls out of French Polynesia must be made via the international operator.

English language newspapers include the Tahiti Sun Press.

MISCELLANEOUS

Local time is GMT — 10

Business Hours
Banks: 7.45 am-3.30 pm Mon-Fri. Some open Saturday 7.45-11.30 am.
Offices: 7.30 am-5 pm Mon-Fri.
Shops: 7.30 am-5 pm Mon-Fri, 7.30-11 am Saturday. Tourist shops open until later.

Electricity is 110 or 220 volts AC 60 cycles.

Credit Cards
American Express is the most widely accepted, with Visa, Mastercard and Diners Club more limited.

Tipping, as with most South Pacific Islands, is not a way of life.

Tahiti has excellent medical and dental services, pharmacies, a large government hospital and several private clinics.

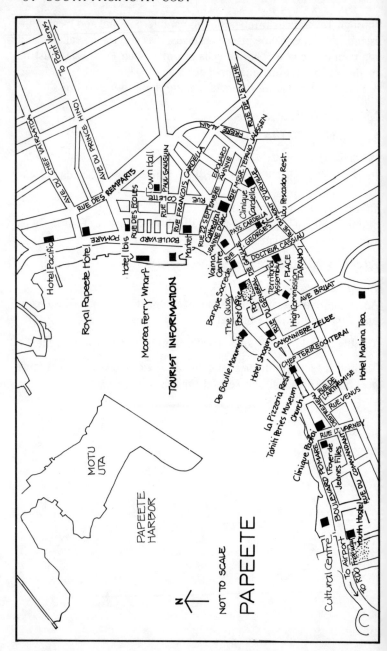

TRAVEL INFORMATION

HOW TO GET THERE

By Air

UTA, Air New Zealand, Lan Chile, Polynesian Airlines and Qantas have frequent flights linking Tahiti with Japan, the west coast of Canada and USA, Hawaii, Samoa, Santiago via Easter Island, Fiji, New Caledonia, Australia, New Zealand, South East Asia and Europe.

By Sea

The international port of Tahiti is served by Chandris, Norwegian America, Holland America, Cunard, Sitmar and Lloyd Triestino. Cruise liners include those from Swedish America and Royal Viking.

TOURIST INFORMATION

Tahiti Tourist Promotion Board Information Centres in Faaa International Airport (where hostesses are on duty at each international arrival) and at Fare Manihini, P.O. Box 65, Papeete, ph 429 626, open daily 7.30am–5pm, Saturday and holidays 8am–4pm. Tourism Committees — Moorea, ph 562 178; Raiatea, ph 662 334; Bora-Bora, ph 677 469; Huahine, ph 682 260.

ACCOMMODATION

The prices indicated here are in French Pacific francs for a double room per night, and should be used as a guide only. A 7% government tax is to be added to the rates.

Tahiti

Deluxe

Sofitel Maeva Beach, P.O. Box 6008, Faaa, ph 428 042 — 8 km (5 miles) west of Papeete and 2.6 km (1.6 miles) from airport — CFP22,500–25,900; Tahara(a, P.O. Box 1015, Papeete, ph 481 122 — 10 km (6 miles) east of Papeete and 14.5 km (9 miles) from airport — CFP20,500–23,600; Tahiti Beachcomber, P.O. Box 6014, Faaa, ph 425 110 — 7 km (4.4 miles) west of Papeete and 1.6 km (1 mile) from airport — CFP22,500–25,900.

Class A
Ibis Belle Fleur, P.O. Box 4545, Papeete, ph 426 621 — 1.6 km (1 mile) from airport and 6.5 km (4 miles) from town centre — CFP10,500; Ibis Papeete, P.O. Box 4545 Papeete, ph 423 277 — on bay front — CFP10,500; Puunui, P.O. Box 7016, Taravae, ph 571 920 — 68 km (41 miles) from Papeete — CFP10,000; Royal Tahitien, P.O. Box 5001, Pirae — 3.2 km (2 miles) from Papeete and 8 km (5 miles) from the airport — CFP13,500.

Class B
Hotel Pacific, P.O. Box 111, Papeete, ph 437 282 — in town centre and 10 mins from airport — CFP6,500-7,500; Hotel Tahiti, P.O. Box 416, Papeete, ph 429 550 — 1.6 km (1 mile) from town centre, 3.2 km (2 miles) from airport — CFP7,500-8,500; Matavai, P.O. Box 32, Papeete, ph 426 767 — town centre and 3.2 km (2 miles) from airport — CFP11,700; Royal Papeete, P.O. Box 919, Papeete, ph 420 129 — town centre — CFP7,500-8,300; Te Puna Bel Air, P.O. Box 6634, Faaa, ph 428 224 — 7.6 km (4.7 miles) west of Papeete and 2 km (1.25 miles) from airport — CFP9,000-11,000.

Moorea (19 km — 12 miles — from Tahiti)

Volcanic crags stand sentinel over pineapple valleys and palm shaded shores. It possesses a storybook landscape with white sandy beaches and a twin bay lagoon. Life operates at vacation pace. By air taxi it is 10 minutes from Tahiti.

Deluxe
Sofitel Kia Ora (bungalow style), P.O. Box 706, Papeete, ph 561 290 — 1.6 km (1 mile) from airport — CFP21,200-24,300; Sofitel Tiare- Moorea, P.O. Box 6008, Papeete — on Opunohu Bay — CFP24,000-31,000.

Class A
Bali Hai Moorea (bungalow style), P.O. Box 26, Moorea, ph 561 359 — 12 km (7.5 miles) from airport — CFP14,000-18,500; Club Bali Hai, P.O. Box 26, Moorea, ph 561 359 — in Cook's Bay, 12 km (7.5 miles) from airport — CFP12,500; Club Med Moorea, 45 minutes from airport, P.O. Box 1010, Papeete, ph 561 500 — CFP11,000 (includes meals); Ibis Moorea, P.O. Box 30, Moorea, ph 561 050 — in Cook's Bay, 7 minute flight from Papeete — CFP10,500; Moorea

Lagoon, P.O. Box 11, Moorea, ph 561 468 — 15 km (9.5 miles) from airport — CFP12,000.

Class B
Captain Cook, P.O. Box 1006, Moorea, ph 561 060; Climat De France Moorea, P.O. Box 1017, Moorea, ph 561 548 — CFP8,000; Kaveka Village, P.O. Box 13, Moorea, ph 561 830 — Cook's Bay — CFP8,000–9,000; Residence Les Tipaniers, Haapiti, Moorea, ph 561 276 — 27 km (17 miles) from airport — CFP10,000; Hotel Hibiscus, P.O. Box 1009, Moorea, ph 561 220 — 27 km (17 miles) from airport — CFP7,500–8,900; Moorea Village, P.O. Box 1008, Moorea, ph 561 002 — 21 km (13 miles) from airport — CFP7,500 (bungalow with kitchen).

Huahine (161 km — 100 miles — from Papeete)

Laboratory for the archeologist, melon garden for the Pacific, mecca for the artist, and a must for the visitor looking for the "as it was" in island culture. Huahine is surprisingly beautiful and has very comfortable accommodation.

Class B
Relais Mahana, P.O. Box 30, Huahine, ph 688 154 — near Parea — CFP11,500; Bali Hai Huahine, ph 561 352 — CFP10,000–14,000; Bellevue, ph 688 276 — CFP4,500.

Raiatea

Once sacred to ancient Polynesia, and sharing the lagoon with the island of Tahaa, it is today's sanctuary to windsurfers, hide-away-isle picnickers and canoe explorers.

First Class, Bungalow Style
Bali Hai Raiatea, P.O. Box 26, Moorea, ph 663 149 — 3.2 km (2 miles) from main town of Uturoa — CFP8,500–15,500.

Bora Bora

This is the ultimate South Pacific Island. Bora Bora has majestic volcanic peaks, a multi-coloured lagoon and some of the most perfect beaches in the world.

Deluxe (Bungalow Style)
Hotel Bora Bora, P.O. Box 1015, Papeete, ph 677 028 — 10 minutes
from village of Vaitape on Point Raititi — CFP23,600–28,900; Sofitel
Marara, P.O. Box 6, Bora Bora, ph 677 046 — CFP23,700–32,000.

Class A
Ibis Bora Bora, P.O. Box 6, Nunue, Bora Bora, ph 677 116 —
CFP10,500–12,500; Club Med, near Vaitape, P.O. Box 575, Papeete,
ph 677 057 — CFP11,000 (includes meals).

Class B
Matira Hotel, P.O. Box 31, Vaitape, BB, ph 677 051 — 6.5 km (4
miles) from village of Vaitape — CFP9600—10,200; Oa Oa Hotel, P.O.
Box 10, Bora Bora, ph 677 084 — 1.6 km (1 mile) from Vaitape —
CFP11,400.

Tetiaroa

Once the summer playground of Tahitian Royalty, 48 km (30 miles)
north of Papeete, this atoll is now owned by Marlon Brando. Realising
the fragile beauty of island ecosystem, he is dedicated to its
preservation.

Tetiaroa Village Hotel (Class B), P.O. Box 2418, Papeete, ph 426 302
— all inclusive air-fare, excursion, room and all meals (2 days/
1 night) CFP37,000.

Rangiroa

Sky Island, the South Pacific's largest atoll, where life on a coral
ribbon of sand under emerald palms is centred on a marine-rich
lagoon.

First Class, (Bungalow Style)
Kia Ora Rangiroa, P.O. Box 706, Papeete, ph 384-Rangiroa — 10
minutes from airport — CFP31,200 (includes meals).

Class B
Bouteille A La Mer, P.O. Box 17, Avatoru, Rangiroa, ph 334-Rangiroa
— CFP20,000 (includes meals); Rangiroa Village, P.O. Box 8,
Avatoru, Rangiroa, ph 383-Rangiroa — CFP14,000 (includes meals).

Manihi

An isolated atoll which is excellent for fishing and scuba diving. Black pearls are farmed in the lagoon.

Kaina Village (Class A), P.O. Box 2460, Papeete, ph 427 553 — CFP27,700 (includes meals).

Rurutu

Rurutu Village (Class B), P.O. Box 6, Unaa, Rurutu, ph 392 — Rurutu, 429 385 — CFP8,500 (includes meals).

Marquesas

Ancient Tikis, tapa cloth, and traditional wood carving — all in a landscape as Herman Melville saw it! 1,419 km (880 miles) north of Tahiti, this cluster of six major islands offers the adventure traveller a Polynesia of tall ships and the painter, Paul Gauguin, is buried on a hill above Atuona. Cruise itineraries or regular air transport with pre-arranged lodgings can be made.

TAHITI

LOCAL TRANSPORT

Air

Local scheduled airline service between Tahiti and other islands of French Polynesia is provided by Air Polynesie, Boulevard Pomare, B.P. 314, Papeete, ph 422 333, 422 222. The aircraft include Britten Norman Islanders, Fokkers Friendship F27 and Twin Otter. The following are the islands served, and flying times.

Moorea — 7 minutes
Hahine — 40 minutes
Raiatea — 45 minutes
Bora-Bora — 50 minutes non-stop, or 1 hour 10 minutes with stop at
            Raiatea.
Maupiti — 20 minutes from Bora-Bora
Rangiroa — 1 hour 5 minutes
Manihi — 2 hours 15 minutes with stop at Rangiroa
Takapoto — 3 hours 10 minutes with stops at Apataki and Arutua
Tubuai — 2 hours 50 minutes with stop at Rurutu
Rurutu — 1 hour 40 minutes
Nuku-Hiva (Marquesas) — 5 hours 5 minutes with stop at Rangiroa
Ua Huka — 35 minutes from Hiva Oa
Hiva Oa — 1 hour 5 minutes from Nuku-Hiva
Ua Pou — 25 minutes from Nuku-Hiva
Anaa — 1 hour 20 minutes
Makemo -- 2 hours 35 minutes with stop at Anaa
Hao — 3 hours 15 minutes with stop at Anaa
Mangareva (Gambiers) — 6 hours 5 minutes
Free baggage allowance on inter-island flights is 22 lbs.

Air Tahiti operates year-round daily services between Tahiti and Moorea by Britten Norman Islander, a Piper Aztec and Twin Otter. Mr. J. Gillot, manager, Box 6019, Faaa, Tahiti, ph 424 429.

Air Taxi Service

Air Polynesie and Air Tahiti serve charters, circle island flights and transportation to other islands in French Polynesia. Transfer from

Faaa International Airport, 3 miles from Papeete is available by bus or taxi. Luggage handling for arriving and departing passengers is free.

Bus

In Tahiti, the famous "le truck" runs an unscheduled bus service between Papeete and outlying districts. It is a good way to meet the Tahitians. Le truck does not circle the island, but operates only between the marketplace in Papeete and the various districts of the island, including the peninsula with Tautira and Teahupoo. There is no set timetable, but they run from early morning until late at night. Pay the driver on the right hand side of the cab as you get off, and shake the dust and rub your sore joints. Definitely for the young.

Taxi

Taxi fares are controlled by the government and displayed in every taxi. Further information is available from the Tahiti Tourist Promotion Board. Taxi ranks are at Station de Jasmin, ph 420 894; Station Vaima, ph 429 835; Station du Marche, ph 420 292 and Station Aeroport, 436 520.

Car

It is possible to rent many makes of cars, by the day or the week, including Fiat, Renault, Peugeot, Volkswagen. The rates for 24 hours vary between 1,000 CFP and 3,800 CFP according to the make of car and whether minimum daily mileage is included. A few names and phone numbers:

Andre, ph 429 404; Avis Polynesie, ph 429 649; Budget, ph 426 645; Eurocar, ph 424 817; Hertz, ph 420 471; Pacificar, ph 424 304; Robert, ph 429 720.

Drivers must be at least 21 years old, and have a driver's license valid for one year. In Tahiti, cars drive on the right hand side of the road.

Moorea Boats

Moorea is linked to Tahiti several times a day by ferries and by speed boat. The voyage takes 35 to 60 minutes and costs from 600 to 1,000 CFP (one way).

EATING OUT

All the tourist hotels have restaurants. In Papeete and around Tahiti, there are also a number of restaurants offering a wide variety of French, Italian, American, Chinese, Vietnamese and Polynesian dishes. Prices for a meal vary from 600 Pacific francs in self-service restaurants to 1,000 Pacific francs and up. Most restaurants stop serving lunch at 2 pm and dinner at 10 pm. All types of liquor and drinks are available in a wide variety of brands. Be sure to sample the local Hinano, Manuia beers and Vaitia non-alcohol beer, all of which are very popular.

The Tahiti Tourist Promotion Board has a booklet listing the restaurants of Tahiti with prices, and it is wise to pick up a copy.

Small restaurants and snack bars are to be found all around the island. Home-style meals are offered at reasonable prices.

Colourful food-wagons called "Les Roulottes" are to be found along the boat dock in Papeete, and they have hot meals and good fast food until very late at night. They even provide bar stools so you can sit and watch the night life. No alcohol is served, but no worries, because there are bars across the street.

There is no shortage of places to go at night, to have a drink and join in the fun, or just to watch others, and the more popular are — Le Chaplin's (music and video clips); Le Palais de la Biere (beers from everywhere); La Retro (in the Vaima Center).

Le Tamure Hut, in the Hotel Royal Papete, has a dinner and Polynesian show on Thursday, Friday and Saturday nights, and is the "in" place in Papeete. For European atmosphere try Le Mayana, ph 428 229 (open Wed–Sat); Paradise, ph 427 305 (free admission); Too Much, in Vaima Center; Club 106, ph 427 292 (free admission); Le Lido, ph 429 584 (young crowd); Bar Lea (open Tues–Sat); La Cave, ph 420 129 (in Hotel Royal Papeete); Le Pitate, ph 428 304 (late starter); Princess Heiata, ph 428 105 (open till 4am weekends).

SHOPPING

The duty free shops are at Faaa International Airport, at the shopping centre Vaima Center in downtown Papeete, and on Boulevard Pomare.

The pareu, Tahiti's national garment can be obtained at the permanent kiosks in the Bougainville Park next to the Papeete Post Office, from stores along the waterfront, in artisan centres around the island, or from hotel boutiques. Why not make your own? Brightly coloured fabrics can be purchased, along with shirts and dresses, at Tahiti Art, Tapa, Magasin Venus and in Chinese shops near the public market.

For locally produced couturier gowns, visit Marie Ah You, Anemone, Aline's, Elegance Tahitienne, Tiare Shop and Vaima Shirts, all in Papeete.

Tahiti's biggest export is the South Seas Black Pearl, and if your budget runs to this type of souvenir, a visit to Tahiti Perles Center in Blvd. Pomare, ph 438 558, would be well worth your while.

On the waterfront in Papeete is an artisan shop, called Matamua, which specialises in wall hangings and tapestries, lampshades, candles, jewellery boxes, paintings and engravings.

Local handicrafts and works of art, basketry, etc. can be purchased almost everywhere around the islands, but in Papeete you might like to visit one or all of the following: Celina Curios, Les Artisans Reunis, Les Tresors des Iles, Manuia Curios, Manuia Junior, Mareva Curios and Polynesian Curios.

A unique and inexpensive souvenir is Monoi Oil, which is made from coconut oil and the essence of flowers, usually the Tiare Tahiti. This can be used as a moisturising lotion, a perfume, suntan lotion, mosquito repellant, hair dressing or a massage lotion, and can be purchased in pharmacies, supermarkets, hotel boutiques and many other shops.

Tahiti's many art galleries are filled with paintings by artists from many parts of the world, including local people with skill and talent. Whether you want to browse or buy, here are a few names and addresses:

Galerie Winkler, ph 428 177, located on rue Jeanne d'Arc between the waterfront street and the Catholic Cathedral; Galerie Vaim'antic, ph 436 896, in the Vaima Center; Galerie Etienne Siquin (Chouchou), ph 420 981, across from the Mandarin Restaurant on rue des Ecoles; Galerie Oviri, ph 426 382, at P.K. 12,700 in Punaauia, on the mountain side, fourth house on the left; Galerie Reva Reva, ph 433 267, 36 rue Lagarde, across the street from the Chinese school; Galerie Du Dragon, rue Clappier above the Bar Taina; Galerie Noa Noa, ph 427 347, on Blvd. Pomare downtown; Fare Manihini, upstairs at the Tahiti Tourist Bureau, which is frequently used for art exhibits.

Pottery works can be purchased directly from the artists' homes. Marlene Robert, an American lady living at P.K. 10 in Punaauia, ph 436 182, works upon order, with 2 exhibits a year and a showroom in her workshop. M.F. Picard sells pottery from her home in Pamatai, ph 425 998.

Diana de Marigny, an American lady who supplied the stained glass windows for the Catholic Cathedral in downtown Papeete, makes stained glass windows at her workshop home, ph 438 337. Dilhan, at P.K. 13,8 in Punaauia, ph 583 260, has a sales room of paintings on velvet by a father and son team.

Yacht base, Papette

SIGHTSEEING

Strolling around Papeete, motoring through rural districts, or touring the neighbouring islands, the visitor can get the same impression of a world that once lured the famous French painer, Paul Gauguin.

Each Sunday from 11.30 am–3 pm, the gardens of OTAC, the Territorial Cultural Centre, are the scene of traditional Polynesia. Beginning with a welcome cocktail, the To'a Tai Brunch gets underway with a barbecue buffet. There are demonstrations of how to wear the pareu, grate a coconut to make coconut milk, and how to prepare "poisson cru", Tahiti's national dish. The Huriama dance group then presents Polynesian songs and dances.

There are special menus served in the restaurant at the Cultural Centre throughout the week. These include Maa Tahiti (Tahitian food) on Wednesday, seafood on Thursday, and a complete Tahitian buffet on Fridays. For information phone Tevaea Amo on 410 650.

Museum of Tahiti and Her Islands is at Pointe des Pecheurs in Punaruu P.K. 17,5, situated in spacious gardens by the sea. Four permanent exhibit halls contain displays and information on the natural environment of the islands, the prehistory and archaeology of the Polynesian settlement process, and their social and religious life, before and after the arrival of the European missionaries. The museum is open daily 9.30 am–5.30 pm, except Monday, ph 583 476. There is an admission fee.

The Lagoonarium, built into the lagoon of Punaauia, at PK 11,4 (7 miles from downtown Papeete), is the largest underwater observatory in a natural environment in the world. Four big fish parks contain several thousand creatures of the sea, and there is an auditorium with several display cases containing the largest seashell collection in Polynesia, plus exhibits of mother-of-pearl and black pearls. Underwater projectors light up the fish parks at night for the diners at the Restaurant Captain Bligh. The Lagoonarium is open daily 9 am–6 pm, ph 436 290, and there is an admission fee.

The Harrison W. Smith Botanical Gardens are located adjacent to the Gauguin Museum in Papeari, 30 miles from Papeete. In these 340 acres there are hundreds of varieties of trees, shrubs, plants and flowers from tropical regions throughout the world. Smith, who died in 1947, was nick-named "Grandfather of the Trees" by the Tahitians. He left his job as a university professor in Boston and devoted his life to creating these botanical gardens. They are open daily, and there is an admission fee.

Any local travel agency (and we have provided a list at the end of this section) can arrange a tour of the island, with or without lunch and/or admissions to the museums for a half or full day. The average tour leaves the hotel at 9.30 am, stopping at One Tree Hill, historic Point Venus, pointing out or stopping at the Blowhole of Arahoho and the Three Cascades of Faarumai. Passing Bougainville's market by the bridge in Hitiaa it continues on to the isthmus of Taravao, where Tahiti-Nui (big Tahiti) connects with Tahiti-Iti (little Tahiti). In Papeari, a visit is made to the Paul Gauguin Museum and Harrison Smith Botanical Gardens, before or after lunch.

The latter half of the tour passes by the Olivier Breaud Golf Course at Atimaono, and stops briefly at the Fern Grotto of Maraa Point. In the communes of Paea and Punaauia there are glimpses of Tahiti's wealthy beachfront properties, often containing old Polynesian style homes built of pandanus and woven bamboo. The multimillion-dollar modern homes are up in the mountains, overlooking Moorea. The full-day tour ends at your hotel, usually around 3.30 or 4 pm.

This tour can be modified to include visits to the Marae of Arahurahu, the Ava Tea Distillery and Tasting Room and the Museum of Tahiti and Her Islands.

The Glass Bottom Boat Tour leaves from Maeva Beach or Beachcomber Hotel, and spends two hours viewing coral gardens, multi-hued lagoon fish, while Tahitian fishermen dive under the boat. Refreshments are provided.

In Gauguin's Footsteps is the name of a tour which retraces the life of the French artist, Paul Gauguin, who lived and painted in Polynesia. Upon his death in 1904 Gauguin was buried in the cemetery of Atuona on the island of Hiva Oa in the Marquesas Archipelago. A morning or afternoon tour takes you through Punaauia, where Gauguin owned land and a house, and tried to commit suicide on a nearby hill; on through Paea to the Grottos of Mara'a, where the artist swam in the pool of the cave; through Papara to Mataiea, where the painter lived for 18 months. The highlight of the tour is a visit to Paul Gauguin Museum in Papeari, which is also a memorial to the life and works of one of the world's most famous painters.

There are also day tours to Bora Bora, Moorea and Tetiaroa, 4WD tours to the inland mountains and valleys, and Helicopter Tours.

Tour Operators
Kia Ora Tours, ph 430 498; Manureva Tours, ph 427 258; Pacific Travel, ph 429 385; Tahiti Nui, ph 426 803/428 550; Tahiti Tours, ph 427 870; Tahiti Poroi, ph 420 070/428 342; Agence Poroi Uturoa, ph 663 318; Tahiti Voyages, ph 425 763; Teremoana Tours, ph 429 696/426 992; Aute Voyages, ph 426 607/425 137; Vahine Tahiti Travel, ph 424 438; Voyagence Tahiti, ph 427 213; Paradise Tours, ph 424 936; Marama Tours, ph 439 581/420 842; Compagnie Maritime Polynesienne, ph 428 402; Bernadette's Bora Bora Day Tours, ph 677 115; Pacific Helicopter Service, ph 431 680; Tahiti Helicoptere Service, ph 433 426.

RECREATION

Golf
The Olivier Breaud International Golf Course is at PK 40,2 in the Communes of Papara and Mataiea, 25 miles from Papeete along the west coast. It was designed by Bob Baldock, a renowned golf architect from California. The course is open daily from 8 am–5 pm, and Golf Tours and Transfers are available Mon-Sat through the Hui Popo company. The pick-up service begins at 8am at the Hotel Hyatt Regency Tahiti, with other pick-ups at the OPATTI office downtown and Hotels Tahiti, Beachcomber, Bel Air and Sofitel Maeva Beach. Departure from the golf course is at 3.30 pm. For further information ph 574 032 or 574 341.

Horseriding
Club Equestre de Tahiti, ph 427 041, is open daily except Monday. Riding is possible in the mountains or by the sea, with breakfast included. Picnic outings upon request.

L'Eperon de Pirae, ph 427 987, is also closed on Mondays, and offers riding in the mountains, a 2-hour seaside ride, including breakfast, and a picnic ride in the mountains for 4–10 people. Lessons available.

Equestrian Center of Hotel Puunui, P.O. Box 7016, Taravao, is located on the grounds of the Hotel Puunui in the mountains of the Tahiti-Iti peninsula. Open daily with four outings per day.

Bowling

Tahiti's only bowling alley is in Arue. Open Tues–Sat, 5pm–1am, Sun 7pm–10pm, closed Mondays. Rental shoes and all necessary equipment available. Restaurant and bar on premises, ph 429 326.

Squash

Hotel Matavai has 2 lighted squash courts, used on a first-come, first-served basis, ph 425 768.

Tennis

Tennis courts are located at the following hotels: Tahiti Beachcomber, Sofitel Maeva Beach, Hyatt Regency Tahiti, Tahiti Country Club, Te Puna Bel Air, Hotel Puunui (on Tahiti-Iti), and at the Tennis Club in Fautaua, ph 420 059. Several more tennis courts exist but they are owned by Sports Clubs and private tennis clubs.

Mountain Climbing

Tahiti Special Excursions can arrange unusual treks for those who wish to explore Tahiti's interior valleys, climb mountains, walk across the island or investigate old lavatubes, burial caves and hidden grottoes. These excursions are classified according to the difficulty, and can take from 1–4 days. For further information phone 437 201. The Alpine Club of Tahiti is headed by Mr Jay. For information phone 481 059.

Deep-Sea Fishing

Haurepe Charters has a 40ft Viking cabin-cruiser "Moetia" accommodating a maximum of 10 passengers for deep-sea fishing or excursions to Moorea, Maiao or Tetiaroa. Based at Fare Ute Marina, ph 428 027.

On the Papeete waterfront there are numerous sport fishing boats for hire. Many of them are represented by the Mer et Loisirs (Sea and Leisure) floating office in front of the Papeete Post Office. Bonito boats are also available for fishing expeditions, using the traditional Tahitian techniques for fishing with bamboo poles. These outings can include a picnic visit to Tetiaroa atoll, to join the "Auroch", which is permanently moored there as a nautical base offering sleeping accommodation for fishing and scuba diving parties, ph 439 799.

Scuba Diving

Tahiti Aquatique Club, owned by American expatriate Richard Johnson, is located at Hotel Sofitel, Maeva Beach. For further information ph 428 042.

Tahiti Plongee (Coral Sub) is based at the Hotel Te Puna Bel Air, with diving programmes for anyone 4–78 years old. Henri Pouliquen is the head of this centre, ph 410 062.

Yacht Club of Tahiti Diving Center is managed by Pascal Le Cointre and Arnaud Demier, both bilingual, highly qualified diving instructors. There are diving outfits for 25 people, and the center organises two dives a day, except on Sunday afternoon, ph 422 355.

Water Skiing

Tahiti Aquatique Club also has water-skiing (see Scuba Diving).

The Nautical Activity Center located at Hotel Te Puna Bel Air is the home of the Ski Nautique Club de Tahiti, a water-skiing association that is open to non-members. For information ph 421 038 or 582 998.

Force 6 is the Watersports Pavilion adjacent to the Hotel Tahiti Beachcomber. Here you can go water-skiing, windsurfing, scuba diving, deep-sea fishing, charter a yacht, take a glass-bottom boat ride, or anything to do with water sports, ph 425 110.

Tahiti Jet Ski Club organises sporting events and open house with demos and equipment testing. In Mataiea, across the road from the Golf Course, ph 574 285.

Surfing

Surf clubs in Tahiti welcome surfing visitors, and will show them where to find the big waves for each season. For information on custom made surboards, surfing conditions and accessories for surf, skate and boogy boards, contact David Kelly at Motu Hana, Regent Paraita St., Papeete, ph 424 539.

Arsene Harehoe also sells and repairs surf boards. He is at P.K. 12,5 in Punaauia, ph 438 691.

Sailing

Sailing vacations can be combined with island hopping, visiting the Leeward Society islands by yacht and flying back to Tahiti, or with scuba diving excursions to the best locations. Contact the following associations for further information:

Sea and Leisure, P.O. Box 3488, Papeete, ph 439 799. This floating office on the Papeete waterfront represents several charter yachts, as well as fishing boats, Hobie Cats, glass bottom boats, surfboards, jet-ski and diving expeditions.

Tahiti Aquatique, c/- Hotel Sofitel Maeva Beach, ph 428 042, has a full line of vessels available, bare boat to skippered, for day sailing or long term charter. These can be combined with scuba diving

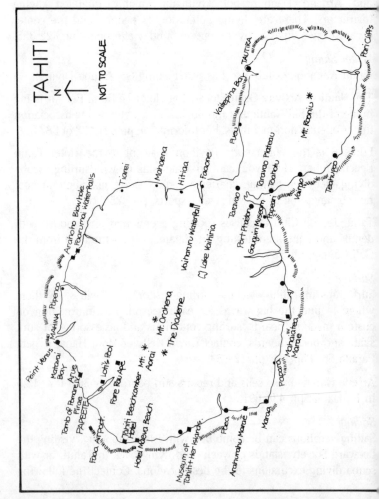

excursions, with a qualified American diving instructor.

Tahiti Cruising Club, P.O. Box 1604, Papeete, ph 426 889, has skippered or bare boat sailing in new or recent yachts ranging from 32 to 83 ft long. Hotel accommodations, airline connections and all other conveniences arranged.

Tahiti Yachting, P.O. Box 363, Papeete, ph 427 803. This 15-year-old company represents a fleet of 6 yachts for charter with or without skipper.

Jacboat, located near the Hotel Maeva Beach "motu", rents small motor boats, with no licence required. Half day rates up to package plans for a weekend. For information ph 421 370.

Spectator Sports
Soccer, the favourite sport of Tahitians, can be seen on almost all of the islands in Polynesia. In Tahiti, crowds gather at the Fautaua Stadium, or the Stade Pater, both located in Pirae, near Papeete, on week nights and during weekends to cheer their team.

As there are many athletic clubs in Tahiti, it is best to call the local newspapers (La Depeche de Tahiti, 424 343) to find out what sporting events are taking place and where.

Horse racing is held on special occasions at the Pirae Hippodrome, where jockeys sometimes ride bareback, wearing only a brightly coloured pareu and a crown of flowers. On-course betting exists, but the payouts are very small.

Outrigger canoe racing is avidly practised, with frequent competitions held to determine the champions of each pirogue club, each community, each island, and finally, which team is the best in Polynesia. These winners then compete for international titles, paddling against teams from Hawaii, California and other Pacific Islands.

Motocross racing is a popular event, with competitions held at the motocross course in Taravao, and in several other parts of the island. There are regular automobile ralleys, bicycle sail-boat races, Delta plane and hang gliding shows, archery competitions, boxing matches, basketball and rugby games and track events.

RAIATEA

Tours and excursions in Raiatea can be arranged through all the small hotels and family pensions. The Hotel Bali Hai is the only first class hotel on the island, with a regular programme of tours to visit the Marae Taputapuatea, the Faaroa River, Tahaa Island and the "motu" islets inside the coral reef.

Raiatea and Tahaa are the vanilla islands of Polynesia. The rich, aroma of vanilla perfumes the air as you drive around these islands during the harvest season. Raiatea, as the second largest island in French Polynesia, has several stores and boutiques in Uturoa, the principal village.

EATING OUT

Restaurants include the Hotel Bali Hai, Le Motu, Jade Garden and the Quai des Pecheurs. You can choose from French, Continental, Chinese or Italian, plus local seafoods and vegetables. Uturoa has several snack bars selling steak and fries, poisson cru and sandwiches.

SIGHTSEEING

One of the most popular excursions on Raiatea is to board an outrigger speed canoe to explore the Faaroa River. This green haven, bordered by wild hibiscus "purau" trees and modern homes, is the historic site where hundreds of Maohi families departed on their migratory voyages to settle in Hawaii and New Zealand. The tour of the Faaroa River, the only navigable river in Tahiti and her Islands, also includes a visit to a nearby "motu" where the visitor can swim, snorkel or just lie on the beach.

A tour to the northwest coast of Raiatea includes a brief stop at the marina, then passes vanilla plantations and continues on to the fishing village of Tevaitoa. Here the Temehani Plateau rises in a formidable wall of basalt, hiding sacred caves behind threads of waterfalls. Marae Tainuu is the main attraction of the tour as it is the largest temple site on this side of Raiatea. A Polynesian sun stone has been found there, plus 10 stones engraved with turtles, depicting a sort of treasure hunt that Maohi warriors had to perform to achieve valour and esteem.

Enclosed within the same lagoon as Raiatea is the island of Tahaa, separated by less than 3 miles, but virtually undiscovered by tourists. Most of the day tours from Raiatea are made by outrigger speed canoe, crossing the protected lagoon in only 30 minutes, and arriving at the village of Tiva.

Marae Taputapuatea is Raiatea's most famous landmark, and was the most important "marae" in eastern Polynesia. Here there is an open-air temple where pre-Christianised Polynesians, the Maohi, worshipped a pantheon of gods. Raiatea was formerly known as Havai'i, the spiritual homeland for the Maohi. This Sacred Island became the cradle of royalty and religion and the centre of culture, history and heraldry.

The sacred passage of Te-Ava-Moa at Opoa offered frequent scenes of grandeur as great double canoes sailed into the lagoon, streaming long pennants from many islands, when delegations from as far away as Rurutu, Tonga and New Zealand arrived to give their respect and sacrifices to Oro, the bloodthirsty war god, who even demanded human offerings.

These pagan rites ended with the arrival of the missionaries.

Red Chevy Tours offer a 4WD excursion that travels through pineapple and vanilla plantations, into the valleys, and to the crest of the mountains. At the Queen's Bathing Pool you can dive from a 15ft overhanging rock into the pool below. The tour ends at the colonial home of Barbara and Chris Zebrowski, beside the Faaroa River.

Tours to visit the Marae Taputapuatea are available upon request, which also includes pies and juice, or Barbara's Silver Service Breakfast. Phone 662 318 (P.O. Box 331, Uturoa, Raiatea) for details.

It is possible to explore Raiatea's past with a professional guide. Johnny Brotherson is an historian and a walking encyclopedia of information about his island. He can give you a comprehensive tour of the seven "marae" temples that comprise Marae Taputapuatea, take you to see the petroglyphs of Tevaitoe, the panoramic view from Mt Tapioi, and help you explore the Faaroa River, re-creating the migratory navigations.

With his outrigger speed canoe that seats 25–30 passengers, Johnny crosses the lagoon to Tahaa, for a complete day tour of this charming island, and a picnic on the "motu". Madame Brotherson operates a family pension at their home in Avera, where Johnny often entertains the guests, recounting legends of Raiatea and tales of witch doctors. His English is very good. For information ph 663 370.

RECREATION

Horseriding
The Kaoha Nui Equestrian Tourism Center, operated by Patrick and Sylvianne Marinthe, has a programme of riding sessions four days a week, including Sundays — P.K. 7, Avera, Raiatea, ph 662 246.

Deep-Sea Fishing
Jeanne-Pierre Constant has half and full-day sport fishing charters aboard his boat "Moana Vaihi", ph 663 683 or 663 097.

Scuba Diving
Raiatea Plongee is owned by Patrice Philip, who speaks English, French and Spanish. The centre has all necessary diving equipment for 12 divers, and there are two daily outings. On Sundays the centre organises a special outing with 2 dives and a picnic lunch.

Lodging for divers is available at Pension Marie-France, who is Patrice's wife, with meals served upon request. For information, P.O. Box 272, Uturoa, Raiatea, ph 663 710.

Walking Tours
For the hiker who wants an overall view of Raiatea and its neighbouring islands, a self-guided round-trip trek to Mount Tapioi takes only 3 hours. The road is not extremely steep, but good walking shoes, water and a camera are necessities.

Then there is the guided tour to find the Tiare Apetahi flower. Polynesian legend claims that the flower represents the five fingers of a beautiful Tahitian vahine who fell in love with the son of a royal chief, and died of a broken heart when she could not marry him because she was a commoner. For information contact Robert Tiatia, Uturoa, ph 662 334.

Sailing
ATM Yachts South Pacific, whose main office is in Paris, have recently moved their nautical base from the Marina Iti on Tahaa to

Faaroa Bay in Raiatea. Managed by Chris and Barbara Zebrowski, the fleet includes 7 sailboats, from 32–47 ft, plus the 50 ft catamaran "Privilege". Bare boat or skippered charters are available, with provisions if desired. For information ph 662 318 (P.O. Box 331, Uturoa, Raiatea).

The Moorings is a marina base on Raiatea with a fleet of 19 yachts, ranging from 37–51 ft for 2–8 passengers. All yachts are equipped with a radio and telephone system. Bare boat or skippered charters are available, and windsurfing and scuba diving equipment can also be rented. P.O. Box 165, Uturoa, Raiatea, ph 663 593.

Association des Professionnels du Tourisme Nautique des Iles Sous-Le-Vent. Members of this group include: 65 ft cruiser "Danae III", 56 ft Columbia ketch "Aita Peapea", 66 ft motor yacht "Manavaroa" and the Moorings fleet. For information — P.O. Box 590, Uturoa, Raiatea, ph 663 593.

TAHAA

For the visitor who chooses to remain a few days on the island of Tahaa, staying in one of the small hotels or family pensions, there are the beaches, but for any organised touring or water activities you have to go to the large hotels. For example the Hotel Restaurant Marina ITI has scuba diving, water-skiing, deep-sea fishing, various sailing programmes, speedboat tours, picnics on the "motu", and excursions to Raiatea, ph 656 101 (P.O. Box 888, Uturoa, Raiatea).

The Hotel Restaurant Hibiscus has sailboat excursions around Tahaa Island, outrigger speed canoe rides, all-day picnics on the "motu" and bicycle rentals. Walking tours are conducted by Andre Lemoine, with a 4-hour hike through the mountains, passing a vanilla plantation and arriving at a lookout point high above the Bay of Hurepiti. Another walk crosses the mountains from Patio to Haamene, with views of nearby Bora Bora, Huahine and Raiatea, plus the five bays of Tahaa below. Night fishing trips can be arranged with the local fishermen. P.O. Box 184, Haamene, Tahaa, ph 656 106.

BORA BORA

Most of the hotels in Bora Bora offer their guests free use of snorkelling equipment and outrigger paddle canoes. The larger hotels have regular demonstrations of pareu tying, making floral crowns and leis, how to prepare "poisson cru", dance the "tamure" or weave baskets and mats. They are society or rainy day games, slide shows, special Happy Hour cocktails with hors d'oeuvres, Tahitian musical entertainment for cocktails and dinner, and barbecue dinners, sometimes served under the stars.

Every hotel on the island can arrange for rental cars, scooters and bicycles, shuttle bus or taxi service to the village or to church on Sunday morning. There arc lagoon outings, picnics on the "motu", shark-feeding expeditions, sailing trips, sunset cruises, scuba diving, deep-sea fishing and circle island tours by lagoon or land, including the Jeep Safari by 4WD Landrover. These activities are handled by concessionaires or by the hotel itself.

EATING OUT

The Beach Bar at Hotel Bora Bora is a popular meeting place for lunch. Hamburgers, Mahi Mahi burgers, Reuben sandwiches on rye, "poisson cru" and huge salads are served. The buffet served each Sunday night in the Matira terrace restaurant features fresh seafoods.

Hotel Moana Beach serves a delicious Mahi Mahi in vanilla sauce, and has barbecue dinners on the beach twice a week, with a champagne and lobster dinner cruise each Wednesday.

Hotel Sofitel Marara has a Tahitian "tamaara'a" each Saturday night, with traditional foods cooked in an underground oven.

Hotel Bora Bora Beach Club serves Gaspacho, California burgers, Mexican tacos, enchiladas and guacamole, plus lasagne for lunch or dinner.

The Yacht Club of Bora Bora, noted for their Bloody Marys and homemade ice cream and sorbets, also serves fresh seafood, including oysters, mussels, scampi, fish soups and grilled lobster. Steak tartare, duck salad and Magret de canard are also favourites.

Hotel Oa Oa has a la carte dining, with selections including steaks,

Mahi Mahi and spaghetti bolognaise.

Hotel Matira has excellent Chinese meals.

Chez Christian at Revatua Club has French cuisine and a good wine list, with seafood specialties.

Bloody Mary's is a popular independent restaurant, with a thatched roof, white sand floor and tables and stools made of coconut logs. Choose your day's catch from a large display of fresh fish, lobster and chicken, and the chef barbecues it on coral stones. The Tupa Bar serves cocktails and appetizers. Free transfers from hotels.

The Blue Lagoon, also independent, is a family affair, with fresh seafoods, and specialising in paella, if notified 24 hours in advance. Transfers from hotels provided.

Some of the popular snack bars around Bora Bora include Leopold's Kaina Snack, where you can get a good hamburger and fries, "poisson cru" and steak. Snack Rofau Beach, near Matira Point, has good prices on breakfast specials, Southern or Kentucky fried chicken, steaks and hamburgers. A small snack bar near the entrance to Matira Beach serves Vietnamese cuisine, and several good snack bars are located in Vaitape village.

Le Recif is the only nightclub on the island, and is open only on weekends.

SHOPPING

The boutiques in Hotels Bora Bora, Moana Beach Bora Bora and Sofitel Marara are well stocked with vacation needs, and include good selections of black pearls. The smaller hotels also have boutiques, with pareus, T-shirts, suntan lotion and film. All around the island you see pareus blowing in the wind, advertising that there is a small boutique nearby.

Alain and Linda is a boutique selling hand-painted pareus and clothing, wall hangings, posters, paintings and black pearl jewellery.

Moana Art features Erwin Christian photography, postcards and books, plus island fashions and black pearls.

Galerie Masson exhibits paintings by the late French artist, Jean Masson and his Tahitian wife, Rosine, who also has her workshop here creating pareus and other items for Bora Bora's beaches.

Naea Studio is in Faanui, with her designs for sale in the Club Revatua boutique. Martine's Boutique sells her hand-painted T-shirts and dresses. The South Seas Pearl shop is located here.

Blue Lagoon has a small boutique and black pearl shop. Bora Bora Pearls is located near the post office in Vaitape. Pofai Shoppe, owned by Hotel Bora Bora, sells souvenir items, Tahitian perfumes and soaps, Tahitian dance costumes, T-shirts and pareus, etc.

Boutique Bamboo in Faanui is small but attractive with pareus, shell jewellery and other local products for sale. Nicholaas Tyburg puts replicas of old sailing ships in bottles and sells them from his home, along with hand fashioned pareus.

The Artisan Center of Bora Bora is located on the quay of Vaitape.

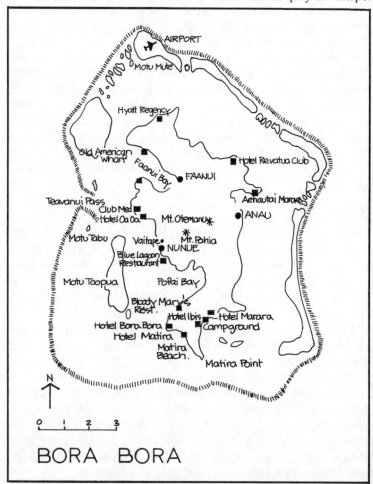

SIGHTSEEING

Circle Island Tours
On the 18-mile circuit of the island you will see modest homes surrounded by flower gardens, small snack stands and little boutiques. The "marae" temples, where Polynesians worshipped in pre-Christian days, are visited, along with the Nissen huts, naval base and heavy artillery guns left behind by the 5,000 American soldiers, sailors and seabees who made a "friendly invasion" of Bora Bora during World War II, leaving behind many blue-eyed children.

These tours are available in the "Le Truck", with English-speaking guides; from Bora Bora Tours at the Hotel Bora Bora (ph 677 028); or from Otemanu Tours, which pick up in front of hotels every afternoon at 2 pm (except Sunday) for a leisurely 2.5 hour tour, ph 677 049.

Vincent Soustrot and his Bora Bora Jeep Safari have a comprehensive tour of the island, which is very popular, but not recommended for the faint-hearted — P.O. Box 264, Vaitape, Bora Bora, ph 677 034.

The Hotel Bora Bora and the Hotel Moana Beach Bora Bora have very relaxing tours in their outrigger sailing canoes, sailing out to the coral gardens and past Point Matira and the basaltic rock called Otemanu (Mountain of Birds). For more details contact either Hotel Bora Bora, P.O. Box 481, Papeete, ph 482 600, or Hotel Moana Beach Bora Bora, P.O. Box 156, Vaitape, Bora Bora, ph 677 373.

Independent operators who offer outrigger canoe trips around the lagoon include: Matira Tours Excursions, P.O. Box 118, Vaitape, Bora Bora, ph 677 097; Hanalei Excursions, P.O. Box 121, Bora Bora, ph 677 470; Bora Bora Aquarium, ph 677 476; Blue Lagoon, P.O. Box 27, Vaitape, Bora Bora, ph 677 054.

Feeding the sharks has become the most popular excursion on Bora Bora, and is easily available for guests in hotels, pensions, campsites or on yachts. There are many variations on the tour, with some operators including a boat trip around the island, picnics on the "motu", reef walking and snorkelling. The tour offered by the Hotel Sofitel Marara includes a three-hour trip around the island, then, donning masks and snorkels, the tourists descend into the clear waters of the warm lagoon, just inside the fringing reef, and walk only a few steps in water about four feet deep until they reach a rope that has been tied around two huge coral heads. The intrepid tourist then kneels on one side of the rope, and the tour guide kneels on the other offering the left-overs from last night's dinner to whatever swims by. Naturally some of the fish don't understand the significance of the rope, but the guide assures everyone that they're more interested in the free food being offered. The sharks are the last to arrive (and it is possible that there is a much smaller audience by the time they make their entrance) but for the die-hards there are usually 40 to 50 Blackfin or Blacktip Reef sharks to see at very close range.

The sharkfeeding show is also presented by: Hotel Moana Beach Bora Bora, Hotel Bora Bora (with Moana Adventure Tours); Bora Bora Beach Club (with the Calypso Club); Revatua Club; Matira Excursions; Blue Lagoon; Hanalei Tours and Bora Bora Aquarium.

A new attraction in Bora Bora is the Galacteus Light Show. This takes place on a "motu" islet inside the coral reef, facing the village of Anau, each Tuesday night. Visitors are transported from their hotels by Le Truck to the jetty at Anau and a boat shaped like a white swan. Crossing the lagoon they go ashore to a theatre under the stars and are entertained by members of a commune, who call themselves Galacteus, and are mostly young French people. They present their original music, fashion designs, comedy and dances from Africa to Asia. A light show features images of the Polynesian sky and the lost continent of Mu, connecting the ancient Lemurians to the Polynesians of today. Books and cassette tapes are for sale after the show. For information contact Galacteus, P.O. Box 161, Bora Bora, ph 677 428.

Catamaran Cruises
The "Taaroa" is a Formula 40 ultra modern racing catamaran based at the Bora Bora Beach Club. A 4-hour sailing excursion departs every morning at 9am sailing in light breezes and shallow waters, right up to the "motu" islands, where the passengers are guided through the jungle to reach the Pacific side of the islet. Here they walk on the living barrier reef, and at a natural aquarium in the lagoon they can snorkel among myriads of fish in only 4 ft of clear water. Fresh water, plastic shoes and face masks are available on board.

"Taaroa" Sunset Cruise: Each evening at 5 pm the "Taaroa" leaves the dock to sail across the lagoon. When the sails are lowered, just after the sun sets, rum punch drinks are served, accompanied by classical music. For information contact Anne-Marie Thomas or Dr Pierre English, P.O. Box 271, Vaitape, Bora Bora, ph 677 046.

"Vehia" Sailing Excursions operate out of the Hotel Bora Bora, managed by Captain Richard Postma, who has been sailing the waters of Polynesia for over 14 years. The "Vehia" Barbecue Picnic Cruise takes place several times a week, leaving at 9.30 am. The "Vehia" Sunset Cruise is legendary at the Hotel Bora Bora. Sailing away from the hotel dock at 5 pm, the boat is usually filled with honeymooners, couples celebrating their anniversaries, lovers and other romantics. P.O., Box 55, Bora Bora, ph 677 079.

Moana Adventure Tours, owned by Erwin Christian, operate out of the Hotel Bora Bora, offering glass-bottom boat rides, barrier reef trips, snorkelling safaris and sharkfeeding, boat trips around the island, airport express speedboat service, speedboat rentals, off-shore fishing, scuba diving, "motu" picnics and a VIP cruise. For information: P.O. Box 5, Vaitape, Bora Bora, ph 677 034; or Hotel Bora Bora (Reservations), P.O. Box 481, Papeete, ph 482 600.

The Calypso Club, based at the Bora Bora Beach Club and headed by Claude Sibani, has water-skiing in all its variations, scuba diving, a snorkelling excursion with sharkfeeding shows and visits around the Bora Bora lagoon. A new 3.5 hour excursion is designed as a lagoon discovery for senior citizens. A covered double canoe takes them around the island, with stops to visit the motu islets and to "play Cousteau" in warm and shallow crystalline lagoon waters, P.O. Box 259, Bora Bora, ph 677 464.

RECREATION

Scuba Diving
Moana Adventure Tours: Certified divers can explore the lagoon depths (up to 50 ft) or dive (up to 80 ft) outside the coral reef. Diving equipment available. Erwin Christian knows all the best diving spots and specialises in underwater photography. Christian is multi-lingual, P.O. Box 5, Vaitape, Bora Bora, ph 677 034.

Calypso Club: Claude Sibani, a diving instructor, gives scuba lessons for beginners and guides certified divers to explore the lagoon and outside barrier reef, P.O. Box 259, Bora Bora, ph 677 464.

Deep-sea Fishing

Aquaholics: Leo Wooten is an expatriate American, whose Japanese wife works with him as deck-hand aboard his twin-diesel 29 ft × 10 ft boat. Equipped with 330 hp and the latest in rods and reels, including 130-80-50 Shimano and International equipment. Can accommodate 4-5 fishermen for half or full day excursions, snacks and beer available, P.O. Box 113, Vaitape, Bora Bora, ph 677 280. Te Aratai II: Owner Keith "Taaroa" Olsen left America 20 years ago for Bora Bora. His boat is a 25 ft Faraillon Fisherman, docked at Hotel Oa Oa in Vaitape. It contains a TMD-40A diesel powered Volvo engine; VHF and CB radio; Everol-Penn International Shimano reels with Sitex fish finder; Pompanette fighting chair and Lee Outriggers. For information: P.O. Box 91, Vaitape, Bora Bora, ph 677 196; or leave message at Restaurant Bloody Mary's. "Mokalei" is a 37 ft Striker with 2 Volvo 165 diesel engines and Penn International 50-80-130 lb line, and 1 fighting chair. Half or full day tours, captained by expatriate American Kirk Pearson, who operates from the Hotel Bora Bora. For information: Hotel Bora Bora, Nunue, Bora Bora, ph 677 028.

"Toerau" is a Fantasy 24 ft equipped with a 155 hp turbo diesel Volvo Penta, with 25 knots cruising speed. Fishing equipment includes 4 Penn International reels, 4 Fenglass 80 lb rods, 2 flying gaffs and 2 professional gaffs. Captain Steve Ellacott is from Bora Bora, and makes his own fishing lures, using ancient Polynesian techniques. P.O. Box 216, Vaitape, Bora Bora, ph 677 063.

Tennis

The Hotel Bora Bora Tennis Club has two regulation tennis courts, with complimentary use of equipment available for hotel guests. This sports complex also includes volleyball and a half basketball court. The Hotel Sofitel Marara has a tennis court, free to hotel guests, to whom priority is given. Arrangements can be made for non-hotel guests to play tennis for a minimal charge.

MOOREA

Most of the hotels in Morea have their own activities programme, which usually include beach towels, outrigger paddle canoes and snorkelling equipment, provided free of charge for hotel guests.

EATING OUT

Moorea has some two dozen restaurants, plus a dozen or more snack bars that serve light meals, sandwiches, crepes, pastries and ice cream. Here we have listed a few.

"Le Bateau" at Residence Linareva is a ferry boat anchored in the lagoon, serving a wide range of cocktails and continental cuisine; L'Oasis is near the Club Med, with Eastern colonial decorations and a large menu; Les Tipaniers has Italian dining and pizzas; The Resto Beach Escargot at Hotel Hibiscus serves French cuisine, fish and seafood specialties; Coconut House in Maharepa has French and Chinese, by the pool; Chez Michel et Jackie is near the Hotel Bali Hai, with a simple setting and a good reputation for its varied meals; Manava Nui has Cantonese and European; Chez Coco Keck's, by the lagoon in Papetoai, has "maa Tahiti" at its best each Sunday; Te Hono Iti, in Cook's Bay is a favourite for lunch.

The Club Med has nightly entertainment of shows, skits and dancing plus a disco, for its quests.

The only other night life on the island, apart from the regular dance shows at the larger hotels, is the weekend activity at Le Tabu, across the road from the Hotel Moorea Lagoon. Each Friday and Saturday night and Sunday afternoon, this new dance hall jumps to a Tahitian beat — music played by a live orchestra in true Polynesian style.

SHOPPING

Moorea, with its many boutiques and artisans, is the fashion leader of island style clothes in Polynesia. The hotel boutiques usually have a good selection, or you can try Island Fashions, Laurie's, Carole Boutique, Shark's Tooth Boutique, Dina's or La Maison Blanche.

Le Petit Village, across the road from Club Med, is small shopping centre with boutiques, perfume shops, curios, and the black pearl shops, Lagon Bleu and Tiki Pearls. The famous pearls can also be purchased at Maohi Pearls, Van Der Heyde Galerie, Island Fashion Pearls, Teva's Moorea Pearl Center and Tropical Aquarium, South Sea Pearls, and in all the hotel boutiques.

Moorea's public market, in Pao Pao beside Cook's Bay, has locally made shell jewellery and hats, baskets and mats woven from palm fronds, pandanus and banana plants.

Galerie Van Der Heyde is on the mountain side facing Cook's Bay, just past the Kaveka Village. In addition to his own vivid paintings of Moorea, Dutchman Aad Van Der Heyde has a collection of carvings, masks and other interesting art work and artifacts from throughout the Pacific. He also wholesales and retails the black pearl. ph 561 422.

Galerie A.P.I is beside the lagoon in Haapiti, before Club Med. It has a year-round exhibit of artistic creations, paintings, water-colours and lithographs. For information contact Patrice Bredel, P.O. Box 1039, Moorea, ph 561 357.

Galerie Martin Roger is in Maharepa, 2 houses down from Banque de Tahiti on the seaside.

SIGHTSEEING

Exploring Moorea can be accomplished by taxi, guided bus tours, rental car, mobylette, vespa and bicycle. Rental agencies are located at the airport, the Vaiare boat dock, in the main tourist areas and at the excursion desks or reception area of the hotels.

A Circle Island Tour takes about 4 hours and includes visits to small villages and views of Moorea's mountains, valleys, lagoons and bays. Stops often include the Catholic Church in Pao Pao, where a nativity scene painted by the late Pierre Heyman portrays the Holy Family as Polynesians.

The Moorea Highlights Tour passes through Opunohu Valley, with its farms, miles of spiky green pineapple plants on the mountain slopes, and grazing cattle. The partially paved road is shaded by acacia trees and bordered by forests of teak, mahogany and Tahitian chestnut trees. This inland tour includes stops to visit Moorea's restored "marae" temples, and archery platforms used by old Polynesian royalty. The bus then climbs high to the Belvedere Lookout Point, for a good view of Moorea, with the two bays of Opunohu and Cook separated by the sacred mountain of Rotui.

Circle Island and Inland Tours can be combined, which often include stops at Teva's Aquarium Centre and the Moorea Distillery and Fruit Juice Factory. For information: Albert Activities Center, P.O. Box 77, Pao Pao, Moorea, ph 561 353; Arii Activities Center, P.O. Box 104, Temae, Moorea, ph 561 286; Benjamin Teraiharoa, Temae, Moorea, ph 561 169; Sandy Germain, Haapiti, Moorea, ph 561 164; Billy Ruta, P.K. 28, Haapiti, Moorea, ph 561 254

Opuhi Plantation is a small botanical garden in the Pao Pao valley, along the road leading to the pineapple plantations, only 5 minutes from the circle island road. The owner, Alex Duprel, speaks many languages.

Teva's Tropical Aquarium Center offers 36 salt water aquariums filled with exotic lagoon fish, sea anemones, live coral, seashells and even moray eels. In addition to the living exhibits of flora and fauna from the Polynesian lagoons, the Center has sales and exhibits of sea-shells, jewellery, sharks' teeth, coral and black pearls, which Teva fashions into creative designs. Open daily. For information — Teva Yrondi, Pao Pao Bay, Moorea, ph 561 912.

The Moorea Distillery and Fruit Juice Factory was built to process the harvests of sweet pineapple that flourish on the slopes of Moorea's mountains. Sold in cartons with no preservatives or additives, the fresh juices contain pineapple, passion-fruit, apples, grapefruit, oranges and limes. A tasting counter offers samples of liqueurs and spirits made from coconut, coffee, carambola, corosol, ginger, guava and mango. P.O. Box 23, Morea, ph 561 133.

Vai Miti Artisan Workshop in Maharepa, near the Hotel Bali Hai, demonstrates how to print a pareu, using engraved blocks of mahogany wood — P.K. 6, Maharepa, Moorea, ph 561 612.

The Tiki Theatre Village is a cultural and folkloric centre built beside the lagoon in Haapiti, past Moorea's hotels and boutiques. Visitors arrive from the sea, transported in outrigger canoes, and are welcomed ashore by a Polynesian chief, who comes out to greet then in his royal canoe, to the sound of conch shells.

Built of bamboo and thatch, the Tiki Theatre Village offers tourists the same Polynesian hospitality that was extended to the 18th century Europeans who first visited these islands.

A traditional dance show is performed and lunch is served at 1 pm.

The village is open daily from 10.30 am–3.30 pm, except Wednesday afternoon.

Each Tuesday and Saturday the Village presents a Tahitian "Tamaara'a Show" with visitors arriving just at sunset. For information contact Olivier Briae, P.O. Box 1016, Moorea, ph 561 086.

Sailing Tours

"Erika", a 19th century 78 ft gaff-rigged ketch, was built in Denmark in 1899 of Danish oak and has been fully restored. Joel House, owner of this red-sailed veteran of the famous Tall Ships Race, offers a 3-hour cruise to Cook's Bay and Opunohu Bay, including a luncheon buffet and guided visit to the Tropical Aquarium Center. Sunset cruises are also available. The "Erika" is based in Pihaena between the two bays. For details contact Mme. Moea Sylvain, P.O. Box 97, Moorea, ph 561 094.

"Esprit", a 50 ft trimaran owned by American David Parkin, is based in Cook's Bay, and every Monday and Thursday takes 4 to 12 passengers from the Hotel Bali Hai and Club Bali Hai on a 3.5 to 4 hour cruise. Leaving at 10am the "Esprit" sails between Cook's Bay and Opunohu Bay, anchoring for snorkelling and lunch on board. Outer island charters are available to Huahine, Raiatea, Tahaa and Bora Bora from March–November for 7–10 days sailing — P.O. Box 111, Temae, Moorea, ph 561 093.

"Kleiner Bar II" is a 36 ft sloop based in Cook's Bay, Moorea, that specialises in out-island sailing charters for a maximum of 4 passengers. Owner Helmuith Hormann caters to German-speaking charterers. For information contact Helmuth, c/- Club Bali Hai, P.O. Box 207, Pao Pao, Moorea, ph 561 368.

"Manu" is a 36 ft catamaran owned by Bernard Calvet, operating out of the Hotel Sofitel Kia Ora Moorea. It specialises in half day sails — Moorea Day Sailing, P.O. Box 96, Moorea, ph 561 255.

"Maraamu II", based at the Papetoai quay near the Bay of Opunohu, is a 62 ft ketch owned by New Zealander Steve Walker, who has 25 years' experience in sailing the waters of Polynesia. The yacht carries 20 passengers for tours in the lagoon of Moorea, and can sleep 8 people for special charters to the Leeward Society Islands. Half and full day cruises are available, with visits ashore to the marae temples and to picnic on a motu islet. Sunset cruises are also available — P.O. Box 1130, Papetoai, Moorea, ph 562 446.

"Seer" is a 70 ft luxury yacht owned by Thierry and Eva Frachon of Moorea Sea and Sun Cruises, based in Cook's Bay. This wooden boat departs each Wednesday morning at 8 am for a sail around Moorea. A 2.5 hours stop is made inside the lagoon for snorkelling, swimming and dining. Beverages are free throughout the day, with a return to port at 5 pm. A Bay to Bay tour with a taste of ocean sailing operates each Monday and Thursday morning. For information: P.O. Box 160, Temae, Moorea, ph 562 501.

Mountain Tours

Bruno Excursions offer guided hikes from the sea to the mountains of Moorea. Bruno Meunier has a selection of treks, according to the ability and desire of his clients, which takes them to the waterfalls, the territorial reservation of agricultural farms, and to climb Moua Puta, the pierced mountain whose summit is often covered by clouds — P.O. Box 97, Moores, ph 561 896.

Moorea Safari Tour is a 4WD drive into the mountains and valleys of Moorea's off-circuit trails. The Landrovers seat 6 passengers maximum and are equipped with A/C, VHF radio and radio-cassette player, plus a first aid kit. The tours depart from the hotels twice daily for 4-hour drives through Opunohu valley into rivers, forests of bamboo, vanilla, coffee and citrus plantations, pineapple fields, and into the government's agricultural area. For information contact Ronald Sage, P.O. Box 1097, Papetoai, Moorea, ph 561 770.

Pacific Helicopter Service have flightseeing tours of Moorea and special flights for aerial photography — Pierre Galipon, P.O. Box 20476, Papeete, ph 431 680.

Lagoon tours and trips to the Motu are available from Lagoon Jet Moorea, P.O. Box 1019, Papetoai, Moorea, ph 561 919. Based at the Hotel Tiare Moorea, they can also arrange for you to waterski, take a ride on a glass-bottom boat, a pedalboat or a small Sea Bob motor boat.

RECREATION

Scuba Diving

Bathy's Club is located at Hotel Tiare Moorea and Bernard Begliomini is the qualified diving instructor. He speaks French and English and can give examinations for B.E. 1st echelon. The centre has daily outings for a maximum of 6 divers, with package programmes that include accommodation and diving discounts. For information: P.O.

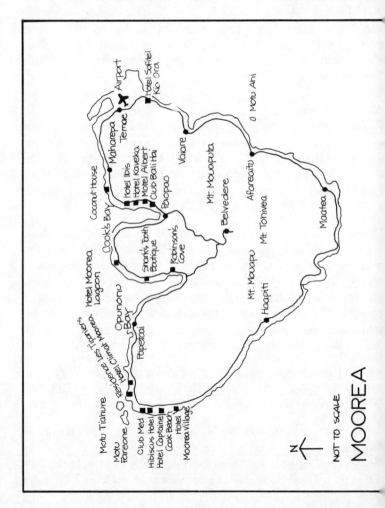

Box 1019, Papetoai, Moorea, ph 561 919.

M.U.S.T. (Moorea Underwater Scuba-diving Tahiti) is located between the Hotel Cook's Bay Moorea and the Hotel Kaveka Village at the edge of Cook's Bay. Philippe Molle is the head of the diving centre, and there are 4 instructors working with him. All are bi-lingual and some speak Spanish also.

The diving centre organises 12 regular dives per week for 12 divers maximum, with two outings per day, except on Mondays, when they are closed. Diving packages include 14 days' complete pension lodging, drinks included, plus 20 dives including equipment. Divers can also stay in the instructor's home, with full pension accommodation. For information: P.O. Box 336, Moorea, ph 561 732.

Scubapiti has its office at the Residence Linareva in the Haapiti district of Moorea. Madame Catherine Arnou is the head of this diving centre, and is qualified as an instructor and Sea Guide. The centre also has two other instructors who are bi-lingual with a minimum level of CMAS** qualifications.

Closed on Wednesdays, Scubapiti organises 2 dives a day the rest of the week, with a maximum of 6 divers. Lodging is available at Residence Linareva, with rates determined according to length of stay and number of dives — P.O. Box 1072, Papetoai, Moorea, ph 562 038.

Tennis

There are tennis courts at the Hotel Sofitel Kia Ora, Hotel Bali Hai, Club Bali Hai, Moorea Lagoon, Tiare Moorea, Moorea Beach Club, Club Med and Moorea Village. These regulation courts also include lights for night matches.

Deep-sea Fishing

All of the sport fishing boats in Tahiti are available for deep-sea fishing around Moorea. Alain Hequet, ph 426 729, specialises in half or full day fishing expeditions in the bountiful waters surrounding Moorea, with his completely outfitted fishing boat.

Horse Riding

Rupe Rupe Ranch is located close to the Club Med in Haapiti. For information about hiring horses for rides along the beach, phone Olivier Ringard on 562 210.

HUAHINE

Tours and excursions can be arranged through the small hotels and pensions, as well as boat trips to visit the lagoon and motu islets, complete with picnics.

EATING OUT

Hotel Bellevue offers excellent local dishes, featuring fresh lagoon fish, lobsters and crabs, plus Chinese cuisine.

The Hotel Huahine Nui restaurant has a new menu including lots of seafood. The chef's specialty is Coquille St. Jacques a la Bretonne.

Relais Mahana near Parea village serves light snacks for lunch and French cuisine for dinner.

Pension Enite is noted for fresh local foods.

The Snackbar Te Marara cooks cheeseburgers and fries, steaks and "poisson cru".

SHOPPING

Besides the boutiques in the hotels and in some of the shops on the island, original creations can be found at The Ranch Workshop at La Petite Ferme.

Paintings on silk, scarves, cushions and "pareus" are on sale at Galerie Matairea'rimai, on the waterfront of Fare.

Local handicrafts include pottery dishes, lamps, vases, hand-painted clothing and jewellery made from mother-of-pearl and seashells.

SIGHTSEEING

A bus tour around Huahine-Nui and Huahine-Iti reveals a Polynesian lifestyle that is still mostly dependent on fishing, raising pigs, coconuts, taro, bananas, coffee, manioc, breadfruit and vanilla beans. Juicy watermelons and cantaloupes are grown on the small coral islets inside the lagoon.

Near the village of Parea on the south end of Huahine-Iti, are some spectacular beaches, excellent snorkelling grounds and more "marae" temples, including ancient petroglyphy. This tour can be arranged by all hotels and pensions.

Maeva Village Archaeological Site
Of all the Polynesian islands Huahine is the richest in archaeological remains. Dr Yoshiko Sinoto of Honolulu's Bishop Museum, has spent many years restoring the Tahitian marae temples of Maeva Village, which is built beside Lake Fauna Nui. This village is an open-air museum, with its stone marae, fish weirs and sacred Matairea Hill lending clues to a civilisation that existed here at least 1,000 years ago. Kings and chiefs lived and worshipped side by side in this royal village, and their proud descendants still carry on some of the traditions. The tour includes a visit to the Fare Pote'e, a replica of a Polynesian meeting house, built on stilts over the lake. For information contact Dorothy Levy, Fare, Huahine, on 688 298.

Gaston Lemaire has a speedboat with an awning that can be used to explore offshore motu islets or to make a tour of Huahine's lagoons. For information — P.O. Box 52, Fare, Huahine, ph 688 114.

RECREATION

The Relais Mahana has tennis, water-skiing, windsurfing, Hobie Cat, pedal-boats, bicycles, ping pong and society games.

Hotel Huahine Nui has a swimming pool, tennis court and marina.

Hotel Bellevue has a swimming pool, table tennis and bocci ball, plus its own minibus for circle island tours and fishing boat for lagoon excursions.

Pension Enite rents bicycles and windsurf boards and has a minibus tour service.

Cars, scooters and bicycles are also for hire through the hotel or from Kake Rent A Car. For information: P.O. Box 34, Fare, Huahine, ph 688 259.

Horse Riding
La Petite Ferme is a ranch with several riding choices — galloping along the beach, exploring the mountains, horseback rides around the island and even camping trips. For information contact Colette Siorat, P.O. Box 12, Fare, Huahine, ph 688298.

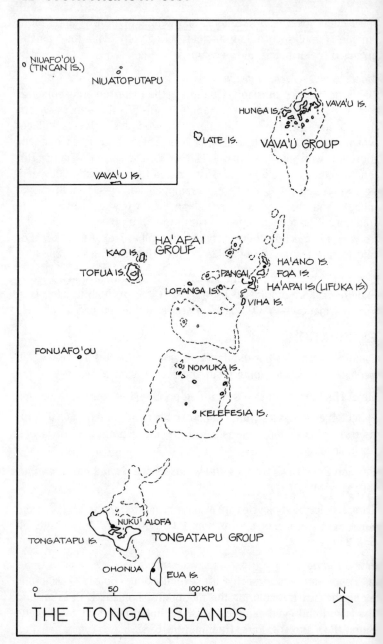

THE TONGA ISLANDS

THE KINGDOM OF TONGA

Tonga consists of 170 islands, 36 of which are inhabited, and is located between latitudes 15S and 23.5S and longitudes 173W and 177W, just below the Tropic of Capricorn and to the West of the International Dateline, south of Samoa and South-east of Fiji. Tonga is the first place in the world to see the sun rise at the dawn of each day, and was formerly known as The Friendly Islands.

The islands are divided into four main groups — Tongatapu, probably the best known with its main town of Nukuàlofa, Eua, Haàpai and Vavaù.

Tonga's present constitution is based on one granted in 1875 and provides for a constitutional monarchy. The executive branch includes the Monarch and the Cabinet; and becomes the Privy Council when presided over by the King.

The Legislative Assembly is made up of seven noble representatives and seven representatives of the people. The King appoints seven Cabinet Ministers who hold office until retirement age. The Governors of Haàpai and Vavaù are appointed to their offices and serve as ex officio members of Cabinets.

There are no political parties in Tonga. The people's representatives in the Legislative Assembly are elected as independents. Three are from Tongatapu; two from Haàpai; and two from Vavaù.

Today's ruling monarch is King Taufaàhau Tupou IV, a direct descendent of King George Tupou I. The King, as his ancestors did, lives on Tongatapu, though the family come from Haàpai, where the King and the Royal Family spend Christmas every year.

HISTORY

Archeologists have established that the islands of Tonga have been settled since at least 500BC, a beginning which today is known only in mythology. It was believed the Tui Tonga, or supreme ruler, was the son of the Creator God Tangaloa Èitumatupuà and his influence was at its height in the 13th century when his domain covered part of the Lau Group in Fiji, Rotuma, Futuna, Ùlvea, Tokelau, Samoa and

Nieu. The collapse of this empire dealt a severe blow to his prestige and authority. The steady growth of population and the resultant control of more and more subjects became a burden that gradually grew heavier. Political unrest followed, and after a series of Tui Tonga assassinations, the 24th Tui Tonga, Kauùlufonuafekai, created the new office of "hau", Temporal Ruler. In 1470, the Tui Tonga, because of his divine origin, became Sacred Ruler.

The first "hau", Moùngamotuà was a younger brother of the Tui Tonga; he founded the dynasty Tuì Haàtakalaua. Later, in the 17th century, the sixth in his line created another dynasty, the Tui'Kanokupolu. Administration of the duties of the three dynasties was carried out throughout the islands by close relatives. The result was a period of peace and prosperity throughout the 16th and 17th centuries.

Captain James Cook made several visits to Tonga in the 1770s, and on his final visit in 1777, he noted that Tongatapu was the residence of Tui Tonga and the other high chiefs. The other islands of the group served as "gardens" and produce from them was despatched to Tongatapu at certain times of the year. Tongatapu was referred to as "Land of Chiefs", and the subordinate islands, "Land of Servants".

"It is a peculiar privilege annexed to the person of the king, not to be punctured (tattooed), nor circumcised . . . as all his subjects are.

"Whenever he walks out, all who meet him must sit down till he has passed. No person is suffered to be over his head; but on the contrary, all must come under his feet. The method of doing homage to him, and the other chiefs, is as follows: the person who is to pay obeisance, squats down before the great personage, and bows the head down to the sole of his foot, which he taps or touches with the under and upper side of the fingers of each hand, then rising up, he retires. We had reason to think, that his majesty cannot refuse anyone who is desirous of paying him this homage, which is called by the natives "moemoe"; for the people would frequently think proper to show him these marks of submission when he was walking; and he was on occasions obliged to stop, and hold up one of his feet behind him; till they had performed this respectful ceremony.

"This, to so corpulent and unwieldly a man as Poulaho, must have been painful and troublesome; and we have sometimes seen him endeavour, by turning to get out of the way, so to reach a convenient place for sitting down."

At the close of the 18th century, in fact just a little after Cook's final visit, Tonga began to feel the rumbles of political change. This culminated in civil war from the 1790s to the 1820s. During the 1820s and 30s two important events were taking place. One, Christianity was struggling to get a foothold in Tonga. Two, there was a struggle for power between Taufaàhau, the young chief of Haàpai and the Tui Tonga and his followers. By 1826, the Wesleyan Mission was effectively established. Taufaàhau was baptised in 1831 and chose the name George, after the King of England. He fought the nobles of Vavaù and destroyed the Tui Tonga of Tongatapu. In 1845 he was proclaimed King George Tupou I, and was able to ensure the loyalty of the nobles of the various islands by giving them land from which they could extract a rental. Aided by Shirley Baker, a Methodist whose statue today stands in Pangai, Hapaài, he was able to ensure independence from British Rule and made Wesleyian the official religion.

With the coming of Christianity Tongan culture began to experience a number of significant changes. Apart from the introduction of a new set of taboos based on the Ten Commandments and the beliefs of Wesleyan Methodism, the missionaries also introduced reading and writing into Tongan culture, so by 1839, it was possible to officially announce a written code of laws — the Code of Vavaù which was limited to the King's subjects in Vavaù. It was not until 1850, at which time the King was acknowledged Ruler of the Islands, that a Code of Laws for the whole of Tonga was in force.

In the 1862 Emancipation Edict, King George abolished the system of semi-serfdom. By 1875 a complete constitution had been drawn up. On May 18, 1900, under the Treaty of Friendship and Protection, Tonga came under British protection. Prior to this there were treaties with France and Germany. Tonga rejoined the comity of nations in June, 1970.

CLIMATE

The climate is very pleasant, being slightly cooler and less humid than most tropical areas. The temperature ranges between 18–25°C (64–77°F) during May through September and 24–32°C (75–90°F) between October and April. Trade winds blow a constant 13-18 knots year round.

POPULATION

The total population of the Kingdom is around 100,000.

LANGUAGE

Tonga has its own language, and here are some words and phrases you will find helpful during your stay.

Hello	Malo e lelei
Good morning	Malo e lelei ki he pongipongi ni
Good evening	Malo e lelei ki he efiafi ni
Welcome	Talitali fiefia
Friend	Kaumeà
Who is it?	Kohai ia?
How do you do?	Fefe hake?
Fine, thank you	Sai pe, Malo
God bye	Àlu a: nofo a (in reply)
How much?	Òku fiha?
How many?	Ko e meà fiha?
Cheap	Maàmaà
Expensive	Mamafa
Go straight	Àlu hangatonu
Turn right	Afe toòmataù
Turn left	Afe toòhema
Stop	Tuù
Go	Àlu
Good	Lelei
Bad	Kovi
Mister	Tangataèiki
Mrs	Fineèiki
Miss	Taàhine
I	Koau
You	Ko koe
We	Òku mau
You (plural)	Ko moutolu
They	Òku nau
Mine	Ààku
Yours	Ààu
Theirs	Ànautolu
One	Taha

Two	Ua
Three	Tolu
Four	Fa
Five	Nima
Six	Ono
Seven	Fitu
Eight	Valu
Nine	Hiva
Ten	Hongofulu
Eleven	Hongofulumataha or Tahataha
Twenty	Uofulu or Uanoa
Twenty-five	Uofulumanima or Uanima
One Hundred	Teau
Thousand	Tahaafe
Ten Thousand	Tahamano
My name is . . .	Ko hoku hingoa ko . . .
come from . . .	Ko èku haù mei . . .
Where is the . . . Hotel	Oku tuù ì fe à e hotele . . .
Police Station	fale polisi
Hospital	falemahaki
Market	maketi
Palace	palasi
Restaurant?	falekai?
When does the boat leave?	Ko e fiha òku folau ai e vaka?
Where is the nearest beach?	Òku tuù ì fe à e matatahi ofi mai ki heni?
Where can I buy . . . ?	Teu fakatau mei fe ha . . . ?
Where is the toilet?	Ko feà e fale malolo?
What is this called?	Ko e ha hono hingoa ò e meà ko èni?
Is it ripe?	Òku momoho?

PUBLIC HOLIDAYS

January 1	New Year's Day.
March–April	Good Friday and Easter Monday.
April 25	Anzac Day.
May 4	Birthday of HRH Crown Prince Tupoutoà.
June 4	Emancipation Day.
July 4	Birthday of HM King Taufaàhau Tupou IV.

Schoolboys, St. Joseph's College, Pangai, Haàpai Islands

An Aussie visitor with friends in front of St. Anthony's Basilica, Nuku'alofa, Tonga

Village life in Fiji

Longboat racing in Tahiti waters

November 4   Constitution Day.
December 4   King Tupou I Day.
December 25   Christmas Day.
December 26   Boxing Day.

ENTRY REGULATIONS

Visitors to Tonga must have a valid passport. No visa is required, but all visitors must have a return ticket.

Duty Free allowance is 1 bottle of spirits and wine and 200 cigarettes per person.

EMBASSIES

Australia:	Australian High Commission, Salote Road, Nukuàlofa, ph 212 244/5.
New Zealand:	NZ High Commission, Tungi Arcade, Taufaàhau Road, Nukuàlofa, ph 21 122
UK:	British High Commission, Vuna Road, Nukuàlofa, ph 21 020/21.
US:	No resident representative. Refer to US Embassy in Fiji, ph 314 446.
Canada:	No resident representative. Refer to High Commission, Wellington, ph 64 (4) 739 577.

MONEY

The local currency is Tongan Paanga or Tongan Dollar, which is equal to 100 Seniti. Notes are in denominations of T$0.5, 1, 2, 5 and 10. Coins are in denominations of T$1 and 2, and 1, 2, 3, 10, 20 and 50 seniti. Approximate rates of exchange are:

A$	=	T$0.87
NZ$	=	$0.75
UK£	=	$1.90
US$	=	$1.00
Can$	=	$0.90

Duty free shopping is available in Tonga, and goods may be purchased with any currency.

You should exchange or spend all your Tongan money before you leave. Tongan denominations are not accepted overseas. In Tonga itself the exchange rate is controlled so you really don't know what your value for money is.

COMMUNICATIONS

The post office is located in Taufaànau Road and is open Mon–Fri 8.30 am–4 pm. If you are a visitor all mail must be collected at the post office. Normally, though, for locals the mail is delivered to the nearest corner store and residents go there to collect their mail. It saves walking to the main street.

IDD services are available and the code for Tonga is 676.

Telegrams and cables can be booked through Cable and Wireless Limited, Tonga.

There is a weekly newspaper, The Chronicle, published in English and Tongan. It is very small and contains little to no international news. With regard to news — newspapers and magazines are obtained from New Zealand and Australia, and invariably are one month old at least. Most expatriates working in Tongatapu go to their embassies to receive current news, of which a summary is telexed through daily.

MISCELLANEOUS

Tonga is 13 hours ahead of Greenwich Mean Time.

Business Hours
Main Stores: Mon–Fri — 8 am–1 pm, 2 pm–5 pm.
             Saturday — 8 am–12 noon.
Banks: Mon–Fri 9.30 am–3.30 pm.
Government Offices: Mon–Fri — 8.30 am–12.30 pm, 1.30 pm–
             4.30 pm.

Electrical supply is 230 volts, AC50 cycles.

There is a tax of T$5.00 when leaving Tonga.

Major credit cards are accepted in major accommodation facilities and by tour operators. Overseas currency may be exchanged at the Bank of Tonga branches.

Tipping is not encouraged in Tonga.

Dress
Men are required to keep the torso covered — T-shirt, shirt but no bare chests.

Many tourists have left the ship to visit Nukuàlofa only to be sent back by Police for not wearing a shirt. The Police are very strict on this. Women should not have the midriff showing. In the islands away from Tongatapu the people themselves, though friendlier, are even more sensitive about this point. It is not unusual to be accosted in the street.

Sunday

On Sunday nothing happens. It is the Lord's Day in Tonga. You cannot swim or play sport, but rather are expected to eat, go to Church and sleep. No shops are open,no services are provided, save transport organised by the hotel to get you to an island away from Tongatapu where there is more freedom.

Many tourists choose to go to the other end of the island to go swimming, snorkelling, etc.

Inter-island ferries moored at Queen Salotte Wharf, Nukuàlofa

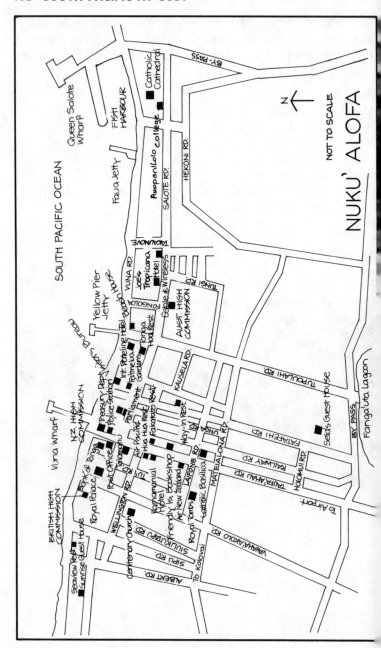

NUKU'ALOFA

TRAVEL INFORMATION

HOW TO GET THERE

By Air
From New Zealand, Air New Zealand and Polynesian Airlines have services direct to Fuaàmotu Airport in Nukuàlofa four times per week.

From Australia Qantas flights are available from Sydney, Melbourne and Brisbane via Fiji twice a week.

The airport is a 45-minute coach drive from downtown Nukuàlofa. The International Dateline Hotel organises transport in an air-conditioned bus to and from the airport for T$7.50 one-way.

By Sea
Most cruise liners call at Tonga, docking either at the Queen Salote Wharf in Nukuàlofa, or the Halaevalu Wharf on Vavaù.

TOURIST INFORMATION

Tonga Visitors' Bureau, Vuna Road (P.O. Box 37), Nukuàlofa, ph 21 733.

Vavaù Office, P.O. Box 18, Neiafu, Vavaù. The staff are very friendly and helpful.There is a tourist publication called "What's On In Tonga".

ACCOMMODATION

There are no international class hotels in Tonga, but there are plenty of beach resorts, guest houses and motels on Tongatapu and the other islands. It is also possible to rent a house by contacting House Rental Agency in the Tungi Arcade, Nukuàlofa (ph 23 092, 9.30am–12 noon).

Here we have listed some accommodation under the various locations. The prices quoted are in Tongan dollars for one night's accommodation, and should be taken as a guide only.

Tongatapu
International Dateline Hotel, P.O. Box 39, Nukuàlofa, ph 21 411 —

0.5 km from centre of seafront — the best hotel on Tongatapu, near international class — $58-67 single room; Ramanial Hotel, P.O. Box 74, Nukuàlofa, ph 21 344 — town centre, has just had a face lift — $46 single room; Friendly Islander Hotel, P.O. Box 142, Nukuàlofa, ph 21 900 — 3 km from town centre — $42 single room.

Joe's Tropicana Hotel, P.O. Box 1169, Nukuàlofa, ph 21 544 — .5 km from town centre — $22 single room; Sela's Guest House, P.O. Box 24, Nukuàlofa, ph 21 430 — 2 km from town centre — $10 single room; Good Samaritan Inn, P.O. Box 36, Nukuàlofa, ph 41 022 — at Kolovai Beach, 18 km from Nukuàlofa — $7-$9 single room; Beach House, P.O. Box 18, Nukuàlofa, ph 21 060 — .6 km from town centre overlooking harbour — $10 single room; Baby Blue Guest House, P.O. Box 249, Nukuàlofa, Ph 22 349 — 3 km from the centre of Nukuàlofa — $8 single room; Fasi-moe-afi Guest House, P.O. Box 316, Nukuàlofa, ph 22 829 — .4 km from town centre — $7-$8 single room; Kimiko's Guest House, P.O. Box 639, Nukuàlofa, ph 22 170 = 1.5 km from town centre — $6-$8 single room; Sunrise Guest House, P.O. Box 132, Nukuàlofa, ph 21 141 — 2 km from town centre at Kolomotuà — $30 single room including meals.

Nukumaànu Motel, P.O. Box 390, Nukuàlofa, ph 21 491 — 2 km from town at Sopu — $35 single room; Way In Motel, Private Bag, Nukuàlofa, ph 21 834 — closest motel to town centre — $15 single room; Moana Motel, P.O. Box 169, Nukuàlofa, ph 21 440 — 2.5 km from town centre overlooking Faua Harbour — $9.50 single.

The Island Resorts

These tend to be the best form of accommodation. Fafa is run by a New Zealander, and it is generally regarded as the best accommodation in the Kingdom. The others listed here are also of a good standard.

Fafa Island Resort, P.O. Box 42, Nukuàlofa, ph 22 800 — 6.4 km north of Nukuàlofa (30 minute launch trip) — $68-$108 single fale (Tongan house); Royal Sunset Island Resort, Nukuàlofa, ph 21 254 — 6.5 miles from town centre — $60 unit; Kahana Lagoon Resort, P.O. Box 137, Nukuàlofa, ph 21 144 — 5 km from town centre — $45 single unit; Pangaimotu Island Resort, P.O. Box 740, Nukuàlofa, ph 22 5888 — 2 km from town centre by boat — $20 single room; Keleti

Beach Resort, P.O. Box 192, Nukuàlofa, ph 21 179 — 10 km from town centre — $14.50 single room.

Èua Island

Fungafonua Motel, P.O. Box 1, Òhohua, Èua — 3 km from Nafanua Wharf — $15 single room; Haukinima Guest House, Futu, Èua — 3 km from Nafanua Wharf — $10 single room.

Vavaù Island

Paradise International Hotel, P.O. Box 11, Neiafu, Vavaù, ph 70 121 — overlooking the Port of Refuge Harbour — $24–$77 single; Tongan Beach Resort, P.O. Box 104, Ùtungake, Vavaù, ph 70 380 — on island of Ùtungake, 9 km from town centre — $32 single room; Stowaway Village, P.O. Box 102, Neiafu, Vava;u, ph 70 137 — 1.5 km from town centre — $7 single room; Vavaù Guest House, P.O. Box 148, Neiafu, ph 70 300 — 1.7 km from town centre — $6 single room; Tufumolou Guest House, Neiafu, Vavaù — 1.5 km from town centre — $6 single room.

Haàpai Island

Haàpai has only a number of guest houses. Lolu, a very helpful Haàpain, runs the Evaloni Guest House.

If you arrive by boat, once off the wharf there is a "restaurant" on the left hand side. Enquire there for accommodation and they will direct you to a guest house. They serve no soft drinks, which you can get from the local trading store, but rather Royal Beer, the local brew — strong and cold.

Fonongavaìnga Guest House, Pangai, Haàpai — 10 minute walk from Taufaàhau Wharf — $10 single room; Evaloni Guest House, Pangai, Haàpai — 5 minute walk from Taufaàhau Wharf — $10 single room; Seletute Guest House, Pangai, Haàpai, ph 60 108 — .6 km from Taufaàhau Wharf — $10 single room.

Niuatoputapu Island

Niuatoputapu Guest House, Hihifo, Niuatoputapu — $12 single room.

LOCAL TRANSPORT

Air

Friendly Islands Airways connects Tongatapu with Vavaù and Haàpai every day. It links with all international air services from Tongatapu.

Twice weekly the local airline flies from Vavaù to Pago Pago, American Samoa.

Sea

MV Olovaha (the Red Boat) and MV Fokulola (the Grey Boat) of the Shipping Corporation of Polynesia run weekly services to Vavaù and Haàpai from Tongatapu. It is best to book when you are there as the times and days can change.

Other privately owned cruising boats and ferries also connect Vavaù with Haàpai and Tongatapu on a frequent basis.

Land

On Tongatapu and Vavaù, land transportation varies from air conditioned buses and taxis to motorcycles (mopeds) bicycles and horses.

Car Hire

The hire of cars is inexpensive. The country has one radar unit, and the speed limit is 40 km/h in town and 65 km/h on the open road. Driving is on the left side of the road. Beware of pigs — they are plentiful. If you hit one besides damage to the car, you can be up for $300 compensation to the owner, who also gets to keep the pig.

Avis Rent A Car have an office in Taufaàhau Road, Nukuàlofa (Ramanlal Hotel Building), ph 21 720, and guests of the Ramanial Hotel may hire cars from the hotel at very competitive rates. There is also a Budget Rent A Car licensee in Taufaàhau Road, ph 23 510.

Licence: Visitors are required to have a valid Tongan driving licence. This is readily obtainable from the Police Traffic Department upon presentation of your current overseas licence. The minimum age to hire a car is 21 years. You have to get into 3 lines — firstly to show your current local licence for a form, secondly to pay the fee, and thirdly to have the licence endorsed by the first officer who issued the form. If you get confused ask the people milling around. The men can be very shy, so the women will probably be of more help.

Rental cars are not available on the other islands.

EATING OUT

The hotels and boarding houses, of course, have dining rooms, and some have cultural floorshows on special nights. There are also restaurants specialising in French, Taiwanese, Japanese or local cuisine. Here are a few examples.

Alice & Andre, Wellington Road; Akiko Restaurant, Taufaàhau Road; Arcade Restaurant, Tuì Road; Fakalato Restaurant, Taufaàhau Road; Fred's Restaurant, Salote Road; Hua-Hua Restaurant, Vuna Road; Seaview Restaurant, Vuna Road.

SHOPPING

Tonga has always been well known for the quality of its handicrafts, but it is now earning a reputation as a competitively low-priced duty-free centre. The range of goods is being added to continuously and offers the visitor a variety of alternatives.

The widest range of duty-free goods is on display in the shopping centre at the Dateline Hotel. Liquor, cigarettes, perfumes, watches, photographic equipment, radios, cassette players and jewellery are available there.

Centrally situated in the main shopping street of Nukuàlofa, the Radio Tonga Duty-Free Store specialises in electronic and electrical equipment.

For the convenience of the last-minute shopper, and for transit passengers, there is a well stocked duty-free store at Fuaàmotu Airport just out of Nuku-alofa.

On cruise ship days in Nukuàlofa, the Duty-Free Store at the Queen Salote Wharf is open for business, as is the store at the Halaevalu Wharf on Vavaù.

There are also a few duty-free centres in Neiafu on Vavaù.

SIGHTSEEING

NUKUÀLOFA

The main points of interest in this town can be seen on a walking tour.

Tuìvakano Residence, Salote Road
This is the home of the Honourable Tuìvakano, Tonga's oldest living nobleman who served in Parliament for many years. The noble's estates include the village of Nukunuku.

The Royal Palace and Chapel
The Victorian white framed Royal Palace and Chapel, surrounded by massive Norfolk pines, dominates the waterfront. The Palace was prefabricated in New Zealand, erected in 1867, and remains unchanged except for the addition of a second storey verandah in 1882 when the Royal Chapel was built. The coronations of King George Tupou II (1893), Queen Salote Tupou III (1918) and King Taufaàhau Tupou IV (1967) have taken place in the Royal Chapel. King George Tupou I was the last king of the Tuì Kanokupolu line to be crowned under the Koka Tree at Hihifo. The Coronation Chair contains a piece of wood from that historic tree.

Visitors are not allowed in the Palace grounds. The small octagonal building named "Palesi" in the corner of the gardens was for many years a rest house for chiefs who were guests of royalty.

Sia-Ko-Veiongo, Salote Road
This is the area to the west of the Palace, and is a Royal Estate. Overlooking the gardens of the Royal Palace, on Mt Zion (also known as Chapel Hill or Zion Hill) is an old home. The hill was the site of the 18th century fortress of Aleamotuà when he was Tuì Kanokupolu. In 1830 the first missionary chapel was built here and a large Wesleyan Church was completed in 1865 under the patronage and supervision of HM King George Tupou I. The former chapel was moved 6.5 km west to the Siaàtoutai Theological College property.

On the crest of the hill may be found the neglected grave of Captain Croker of the British sloop HMS Favourite, who was killed at Pea on June 24, 1840, when he and his men attacked the fortress.

Àhomeè's Residence, Taufaàhau Road
The home of Tongan noble Honourable Àhomeè, whose chiefly

Tongatapu's main road to the Airport

ancestor, Tevita Àhomeè offered up the first prayer before a congregation of almost 5,000 gathered to celebrate Emancipation Day, June 4, 1862, following the promulgation of the Code of 1862. This Code formed the basis of the present Constitution.

Niukasa", Vuna Road
Setaleki Mumui, a Tongan nobleman of the 19th century, sailed several times to Britain where he stayed with friends in Newcastle. On his final return to Tonga, Mumui (who was the son of the Tuì Kanokupolu, Tupou Malohi) built this house on royal land and named it "Niukasa" which is a direct Tonganization of his favourite city, Newcastle. It has been a private residence since the death of the last of Mumuiŝ heirs in 1960.

The British High Commissioner's Residence, Vuna Road
Situated on the left of the Palace, facing the sea, it was originally owned by Motekiai Halaholo and his wife, Sisilia Tupou, and was given to the government in exchange for a waterfront lot at Kolomotuà about the turn of the century. In 1901 it was leased to the British Government for use by its senior representative. Set in spacious grounds overlooking the waterfront, its flag-pole is surrounded by four cannon from the ill fated "Port au Prince", wrecked off Haàpai in 1806.

"Malaèàloa", Vuna Road

The name of this cemetery is derived from Malaè — meaning field — and loa — difficulty or tragedy. The area is fenced with toa (casuarina) trees. The site was especially selected as a chiefly burial ground. The wife of HM King George Tupou I, Queen Lupe Pauù (Charlotte) and Queen Takipois, second wife of King George II are buried here. The first to be buried in this cemetery was the Tuì Kanokupolu Mumui.

"Ovalau", Vuna Road

This weatherboard residence was built in Levuka, the old capital of Fiji, and shipped to Tonga and re-erected on its present site in the early 1950s. It was occupied by the manager of the old trading company of Morris Hedstrom until the manager moved to new company quarters in Sopu. This building is now leased to the New Zealand Government for use as a High Commission senior staff residence.

"Faiàkoka", Vuna Road

The earliest connections of this house appear to be with the noble Veèhala's family. Later it was occupied by a British Consular Representative. More recently it was used as government quarters. The late Queen Salote lived in this house during the Royal Visit of HM Queen Elizabeth II so that the Queen and Prince Philip could stay in the Royal Palace. In 1976, when the property was leased to the New Zealand government as a residence for its High Commissioner, the building and grounds were in a very neglected state. The property has since been restored to much of its former glory.

Cecil Cocker's Residence, Wellington Road

The oldest part of this house was built in approximately 1880. The builder was the son of the first British Consul, Joshua Cocker. The house was re-constructed by Joshua's son, James, in 1925. His son, Cecil Cocker, who is a senior civil servant, lives here with his family.

Opposite Mr Cocker's house (to the west) is "Faletuùloto", the residence of the Chief Tuìtavake.

President's House, Free Wesleyan Church of Tonga, Wellington Road

Believed to have been built about 1871 for the Rev. Shirley Baker, this impressive mansion has been the home of successive Presidents of the Wesleyan Church in Tonga. It is best viewed from the grounds of the adjoining Centenary church.

The Centenary Church, Wellington Road
This building took three years to complete, and was opened by HM Queen Salote Tupou III in 1952. Measuring 56.8 m by 21.3 m it seats over 2,000.

"Otualea", Wellington Road
Originally part of the Palace grounds, this area was known as "Kai Pongipongi" (breakfast) as this was where the people who worked and lived in the Palace had their meals.

The name of the house comes from the beach of Òtualea in Vavaù, and was originally a government house which was given to Siaosa Tukuàho, an uncle of the late Queen Salote, in an exchange of properties. The reason for the exchange was that the expatriate officials living there complained about the many neighbouring church bells ringing in the early hours of the morning. The house was extensively rebuilt in 1946 to accommodate Her Majesty's relatives coming to Nukuàlofa for the double wedding of her sons, Prince Tungi (now HM King Taufaàhau Tupou IV) and Prince Fatafehi Tuìpelehake (presently Prime Minister of the Kingdom).

The Old Free Wesleyan Church
This classic example of early Tongan church architecture was built in 1888 and accommodated 800 worshippers. It was originally erected on the site of the present Centenary Church, but was moved to its existing position in 1949.

"Malaèkula"
This area was named after the Katoanga Kula Festival organised by HM King George Tupou I and held here in 1885. The Tongan National Anthem was first publicly performed here during the festival.

These large park-like grounds are sacred now to all Tongans as the burial ground for Royalty since 1893. At one time the grounds surrounding the Royal Tombs were used as a golf course. Nowadays the sight of royal cows grazing there is more common.

Queen Salote College, Mateialona Road
Between 1875–1879 large sums of money were raised to celebrate the Golden Jubilee of the Wesleyan Church in Tonga (1876). These funds

provided for the building of 5 new churches. King George Tupou I also requested the fund to build a Ladies' College to be known as Queen Charlotte's College, in honour of his wife. However, for reasons not now clear, it was not until 1923 that a separate Ladies' College was established from the nucleus of the girl's section of Tupou College, and later named Queen Salote College.

Queen Salote Memorial Hall, Mateialona Road
In 1966, as a mark of love and respect for their late monarch, HM Queen Salote Tupou III, the people of Tonga raised funds for the construction of a memorial hall on government land adjacent to Tonga High School. A design was selected and work commenced, but unfortunately someone in authority absconded with the funds, and the hall has never been completed. It lies derelict and overgrown.

Anglican Church
Founded in Tonga by Shirley Baker after he was dismissed from the Wesleyan Church, and later the Free Church of Tonga, the Anglican Church was established here in 1900 under licence from Bishop Willis of Dunedin, New Zealand. The present church was completed in 1929-30 as a memorial to Dr Alfred Willis, DD, who was assistant Bishop of Tonga 1902-1920.

Talamahu Market, Salote Road
The market is built on the site of the Queen Victoria Hall — a social centre in Nukuàlofa for many years. Open every day except Sunday, it has a number of handicraft and souvenir stalls, as well as cheap fruit and vegetables.

"Fatai", Vuna Road
The sea-front residence of HRH Prince Tuìpelehake, Prime Minister of the Kingdom, is on land originally owned by his grandparents. During her last period of illness, the late Queen Salote lived in "Fatai" as she could no longer manage the stairs in the Palace.

Vuna Market, Vuna Road
Originally the Customs House stood on this site opposite the Treasury building. The market was constructed in 1955, for the sale of fruit, vegetables and meat. Because supplies of local meat are irregular, a sign outside the market indicates the type of meat available each day. Adjacent is the roadside fish market.

Vuna Wharf

Constructed in 1906, Vuna Wharf was enlarged in 1933 and improved over the years. It was the arrival point in Tonga for many thousands of visitors over the next six decades, however, changing requirements created the need for a modern wharf facility, and the Queen Salote Wharf was built at Maùfanga in 1965. In 1977 earthquake extensively damaged Vuna Wharf and it remains unsafe and unused, except for emergencies.

St Mary's Cathedral, Vuna Road

Built in classic Tongan architectural style of high roof and comparatively short walls, this Catholic Cathedral is the most beautiful building in Nukuàlofa. Financed and built by the Catholics on the island, it is situated opposite Queen Salote Wharf and is worth a visit.

"Langa Fonua", Taufaàhau Road

William (Viliami) Cocker built this house for his five daughters who lived in New Zealand and came to Nukuàlofa every winter. This old residence is now the headquarters of Langa Fonua, a women's co-operative movement, founded in 1953 by Queen Salote with the aims of improving living conditions in the villages and the fostering of handicrafts. The late Queen was President until her death, and the present President is Queen Mataàho. The association was established, and is still operated, entirely by women.

Basilica of St Anthony of Padua, Laifone Road

The first Basilica in the South Pacific, this magnificent building was opened on January 8, 1980 by HM King Taufaàhau Tupou IV. The two storey circular building is 36 m in diameter and 29 m in height, and was built by the local people without the use of cranes. Even youngsters were involved. Beneath the Basilica is a well-equipped community centre and a Japanese tea-room open to the public.

Outlying Attractions

Tongan National Centre

Situated on the main road to the Airport, 3 km from Nukuàlofa, this new centre is set out like an old Tongan village and has an amphitheatre, education centre, exhibition centre and fales (native houses) where visitors can watch tapa and canoe making, wood carving, basket and mat weaving. The centre features Kava

Wharf scene, Pangai, Haàpai group

Typical island bay, Haàpai group

ceremonies and Umu Feasts (earth oven) and there are plans for a restaurant to be built with views out over the lagoon, a traditional fishing ground.

Blow Holes
14.5 km (9 miles) from Nukuàlofa on the coastline at Houma, there are a series of holes in the coral reef, through which the seawater spurts up to 18 m into the air. The area is locally known as "Mapu à Vaea (the Chief's Whistle) because of the sound caused by the gushing water.

If sailing on that side of the island, one can see the spectacular sight of a coastline of blow holes spurting forth.

If walking near the blow holes care should be taken as the coral is sharp, and cuts are hard to clean and can lead to infections. Always wear sturdy shoes. Also a number of tourists have been washed off the rocks because of carelessness, and have drowned. There are no lifesavers or coastal patrol boats. It would take over half a day to get a boat to the area from the other side of the island, and it is impossible to clamber back onto the rocks.

Flying Foxes
18 km (11 miles) from Nukuàlofa at Kolovai, are trees literally filled to capacity with flying foxes, some of which have a wing span up to 1m.

Haàmonga Trilithon
Although Nukuàlofa has been the seat of government and the royal family for over a century now, legend records that the first Tongan kings ruled from the far Eastern village of Niutoua, where the monumental Haàmonga (trilithon) stone stands. This trilithon consists of two large vertical stones with a third horizontal connecting stone mortised into the tops of the upright pillars.

These uprights are about 5 m high, 4.25 m wide and 1.4m thick. The lintel is 5.8 m long, 1.4 m wide and 0.61 m thick. The visible portions of the uprights are estimated to weigh between 30 and 40 tonnes each.

The eleventh Tuì Tonga, Tuìtatui, built the trilithon about 1200AD.

Lapaha
9 km (5 miles) from Nukuàlofa on the shores of a lagoon is Lapaha, the northern district of Muà. Because it was the centre of Tongan

culture and rulers for at least six centuries, it is the richest area for archaeological monuments in the Kingdom.

COMMENT. The roads are few, the sights are well signposted, so if you wish to do something different and get lost occasionally, hire a moped or bike. You can always ask the locals where to go, but you must do so in such a way that they give you the answer you need. Otherwise they will always agree so as not to offend, and you end up lost elsewhere. Most of the older people do not speak English, but Tongan. The school children and younger people understand English.

VAVAÙ

There is a guide book available from the Visitors' Bureau which has 43 pages crammed with information on places to see and things to do in this interesting harbour town of nearly 5,000 inhabitants. Here are a few places you should not miss.

Fangatongo
Along Fatafehi Road, past the Vavaù Club and the European cemetery is the Fangatongo Royal Residence. From here there is a beautiful view of the Port-Of-Refuge Harbour and part of the Archipelago.

Mt Talau
A steep path past the St. Peter Chanel Chapel (named after the French priest who visited Vavaù in 1837 and was martyred in Wallis Island) leads to the summit and a glorious view of the town, harbour and other islands in the group.

Sailoame Market
Here there is a cornucopia of tropical fruit and delicacies. Try limu fuofua, made from tasty seaweed, and ifi, roasted Tahitian chestnuts.

HAÀPAI

The island is flat like Tongatapu, but has a far fresher feel: the houses are better kept, and the people friendlier.

Pangai
This is the main town and houses the local general and merchant store, police station, a variety of schools — Tongan Church, Catholic — and hospital.

A young couple somewhere in the South Pacific

The Pangai shoreline has two jetties, and there are many small fishing vessels. The place does not boast of "organised" fishing trips. All you need to do is to enquire at the local store or the restaurant, and they will organise a trip for you. There is a local bus, of sorts, that goes up and down the island from the transmission station at one end, to the causeway at the other. The causeway was built by the Kiwi Army some years ago to link Foa Island with Haàpai.

King's Residence
The present King of Tonga was born here in the home of the present

Royal Palace, Nukuàlofa

dynasty. Each Christmas the Tongan Royal Family retire to Haàpai to celebrate the feast day, and spend their holidays. The house is of typical European construction — wooden with enclosed verandahs. The gardens extend to the shore, and clearly it is the best house on the island.

Volcano

From the township of Pangai at night, you can see on one of the nearby islands, the molten lava of a "live" volcano. Its red and purple colours, ever changing, are in stark contrast to the dark of night, lit only by myriads of stars overhead.

The Villages

Life on Haàpai is extremely tranquil. A few cars, the laughter of children in class, the snorting of the ever-present pigs, the chatter at the local market, the tolling of church bells at appointed times daily, the shouting of rugby players, these are the sounds of Haàpai.

Villages are poor, but the people are cheerful. On the way out of Pangai on the right hand side of the road, in a cemetery Tongan style appears a "Churchillesque" type statue. It is the tomb of Shirley Baker, a controversial protestant minister who changed religions 3 times and was instrumental in the fortunes of the present royal dynasty in the 19th century.

Swimming and Snorkelling

With advice from the people at the guest house, you can get one of the local fishermen to organise an outing. Negotiate the deal with the guest house owner. Everything is informal. They'll ensure you have a great time, and will take you to a nearby island, some forty minutes away, protected by reefs where you can snorkel and swim in safety.

Foa

This is another tree-lined tropical paradise. It has brilliant sandy beaches lapped by the aqua coloured water of the Pacific. All the islands are surrounded by coral reefs. Foa is adjacent to another island which can be reached by good swimmers. There is no rip, as some 100 m off shore is a coral reef bounding the lagoon. However, you must always wear shoes as the coral is sharp and can cut your feet severely.

Transport — well, get the bus to the causeway and then settle down for an hour's tramp to the beach — but it is worth it.

TORRES
ISLANDS

HIU
TEGUA
LO
TOGA   URPARAPARA

VANUA LAVA   VALUA
MOTA

BANKS
ISLANDS   GAUA (SANTA MARIA)

MERE LAVA

SAKAU

ESPIRITU
SANTO   AOBA   MAEWO

SANTO   PALLIOLA

MALO   PENTECOST

NORSUP
LAKATORO   AMBRYM

MALEKULA   PAAMA
LOPEVI

LAMAP   EPI

TONGOA

EMAE
SHEPHERD GROUP   MAKURA
MATASO

NGUNA
MOSO
HAT   EFATE
PORT VILA

ERROMANGO
COOK BAY

ANIWA

LENAKEL   SULPHUR
BAY   FUTUNA

ANEITYUM

N

NOT TO SCALE

VANUATU

VANUATU

Vanuatu is a group of 80 islands north-east of New Caledonia, ruled as an independent republic by its own indigenous people. It lies 2,500 km (1,550 miles) north-east of Sydney, 2,000 km (1,240 miles) north of Auckland, 800 km (496 miles) west of Fiji and 400 km (248 miles) north-east of New Caledonia.

Formerly known as the New Hebrides, the islands are volcanic in origin and stretch north to south-east for about 900 km (558 miles). Most of the islands have narrow bands of cultivated land along the coasts with densely forested and mountainous interiors. There are five active volcanoes in the group.

The main islands of the group are Espiritu Santo (the largest), Efate (which contains the capital Port Vila), Tanna, Malakula, Ambrym, Pentecost, Epi, Erromango, Anatom, Aoba and Aniwa (the smallest).

HISTORY

It is thought that Vanuatu was settled about 5,000 years ago, and while the origins of the settlers are unclear, they were probably Melanesian. They developed a culture rich in stories and legends, customs and rituals. They also introduced a wide variety of food crops and animals and at some point in time, pigs, which became most important, for their ownership was indicative of wealth. When the upper incisors of the pig are knocked out and the animal is hand-fed cooked food for seven to ten years, full circle tusks develop and these, too, became a symbol of wealth.

Communities were separated by dense jungle, rugged volcanic terrain and expanses of ocean. Because of the nature of their land, these original settlers had an unshakeable belief in the power of the spirits, and traditions filtered through the islands while others evolved in separate and unique ways. Separation from each other led to fear and hostilities.

Open warfare rarely, if ever, existed — but sporadic killing, wife-stealing and cannibalism were common.

In May 1606, de Quiros landed in Big Bay on Espiritu Santo, mistaking it for Terra Australis Incognita (Australia). The Spanish declared the country theirs in the name of Spain and God. In 1786 Bougainville sailed through, and six years later James Cook discovered the full extent of the islands, naming them the New Hebrides.

Australian sandalwood traders soon followed, introducing ravaging diseases which rapidly decimated the local population. The traders were a lawless breed who would not hesitate to kill the natives who stood between them and their precious cargo. When sandalwood prices were down, they turned their attention to biche-de-mer (sea cucumbers), pearls, turtle shell and whales. Meanwhile, the missionaries decided Vanuatu should be Christianised, but their first two emissaries were killed. Within the next 25 years a few more were killed, and Vanuatu, along with Fiji, became known as the Cannibal Islands.

Nevertheless, Christianity won through, but maybe not in quite the way it was intended. People mingled old customs with the new religion, believing in both God and spirits, ghosts, sorcery and magic. In 1860 the Australian sugar industry based in Queensland needed cheap and reliable labour. Recruits were found in Vanuatu, either by indentured contracts or by outright slavery. Many were never to see home again, dying either on the recruiter's decrepit ships, or on the cane fields. Others adjusted to life in Queensland and remained as free men. Those who returned introduced changes to their culture, and a new language — bislama. This pidgin English was their only form of communication amongst themselves and their white overseers. Though its origins are obscure, "bislama" is derived from the words "biche-de-mer", and is now the official language of Vanuatu.

By the late 1800s, France decided it wanted Vanuatu as a colony. The British had little interest in it, although Australian traders did. The Protestant missionaries hated French Catholicism and lobbied the British Government to annex the islands.

In April 1904, a politically expedient but patently ridiculous compromise was reached whereby both governments would jointly rule the New Hebrides as a condominium. Usually referred to as the "pandemonium", it satisfied nobody, least of all the indigenous population.

Them came World War II, and with it the Americans. White men and negroes were seen working side by side, and the Americans' obvious materialism left a lasting impression on the people, precipitating the development of cargo cults, like the John Frumms of Tanna. After the war, villages formed co-operatives, forcing the Europeans into cattle production in order to make money. This necessitated the "purchase" of land from the owners, who thought they were only selling the rights of use. Such events led the people towards an overt desire for independence.

By the late 1970s the foundations had been laid for the election of their own government, and in November 1979, Father Walter Lini of the Vanuatu Party emerged the ultimate leader. In July 1980, the new Hebrides became Vanuatu, and independent.

In November 1983, Lini's government was re-elected with a reduced majority. It has suffered a few teething problems, but it is clear that the people of this new nation are determined to make their way in the world on their own terms.

CLIMATE

Summer is from November to March with an average temperature of 28°C (82°F). Winter is from May to October — average 23°C (73°F).

Light and casual dress is recommended, but not too brief especially outside your hotel. Tropical clothes for evening wear, open necked shirts, no ties.

POPULATION

Melanesian inhabitants born in Vanuatu are called ni-Vanuatu. A number of Australians, New Zealanders and Europeans are involved in the tourist industry, business and commerce. The country's total population is approximately 130,000.

LANGUAGE

English and French are widely spoken, with Bislama being the official language. Following are a few words in Bislama (pidgin) which are included more for entertainment than anything else.

I or me	Mi
Us	Yumi
You	Yufala
You (two people)	Yutufala
You (three people)	Yutrifala
My name	Nem blong mi

My wife's name	Nem blong misis blong mi
Hello	Gudmoning or gudnaet
Goodbye	Tata
How much is this?	Wanem praes blong hem?
Later	Bambae
Earlier	Bifo
I don't understand	Mi no save

PUBLIC HOLIDAYS

January 1	New Year's Day
March 5	National Chief's Day
March/April	Good Friday/Easter Monday
May 1	Labour Day
July 30	Independence Day
August 15	Assumption Day
October 5	Constitution Day
November 29	Unity Day
December 25	Christmas Day
December 26	Family Day

The two great holidays of the old condominium, Bastille Day and Queen's Birthday, are no longer publicly celebrated.

ENTRY REGULATIONS

A valid passport is required, but a visa is not necessary. The duty free allowance for visitors over 18 years is 200 cigarettes or 250g tobacco or 50 cigars, 1.5 litre liquor or two bottles wine, quarter litre eau de toilette, 10cl perfume and all personal effects, cameras and film.

EMBASSIES

Australia:	Australian High Commission, Melitco House, Port Vila, ph 2 777.
New Zealand:	NZ High Commission, Prouds Building, Kumul Highway, Port Vila, ph 2 933.
US:	No resident representative. Refer to US Embassy in Wellington, NZ, ph 64 (4) 722 068.
UK:	British High Commission, Melitco House, rue Pasteur, Vila, ph 3 100.
Canada:	Canadian High Commission in Australia, ph (062) 73 3844, is accredited to Vanuatu.

MONEY

Even when it was the Condominium of the New Hebrides, Vanuatu had two official currencies, circulating side by side, as legal tender. They were the New Hebrides Franc (based on the French Franc), and the Australian Dollar. While confusing to visitors, it had the effect of making locals — and especially merchants dealing with money on a day-do-day basis — highly skilled at translating prices from one currency to the other. To this day that skill remains. When independence came in 1979, a new currency, called "vatu", was introduced.

To the visitor, shopping in Vanuatu can be confusing, because of the profusion of exchange rates and currencies flowing freely into the country, the latter the result of Vanuatu's liberal attitude to exchange controls, and income tax.

To attract sales, shops and restaurants in Vanuatu frequently offer considerably different exchange rates for cash and travellers cheques, effectively giving tourists a discount. Visitors should therefore refrain from cashing all their travellers cheques when they first arrive.

The local expertise in dealing with two currencies makes it possible for Vanuatu merchants to very quickly calculate exchange rates, and provide change in one currency or the other so quickly that visitors are sometimes convinced they are being cheated.

Notes are in denominations of VT100, 500 and 1,000. Coins (Centimes) are in denominations of 1, 2, 5, 10, 20 and 50. 1 Vatu = 100 Centimes.

Approximate rates of exchange are:

A$	=	VT88
NZ$	=	67
UK£	=	183
US$	=	108
Can$	=	91

COMMUNICATIONS

IDD telecommunications, telex and FAX are available from Vanuatu to anywhere in the world, 24 hours per day, seven days per week. The country code is 678.

The government issues a tri-lingual weekly newspaper once called Tam Tam and now entitled Vanuatu Weekly — Hebdomadaire. A free tourist publication, What to do in Vanuatu, is issued irregularly and

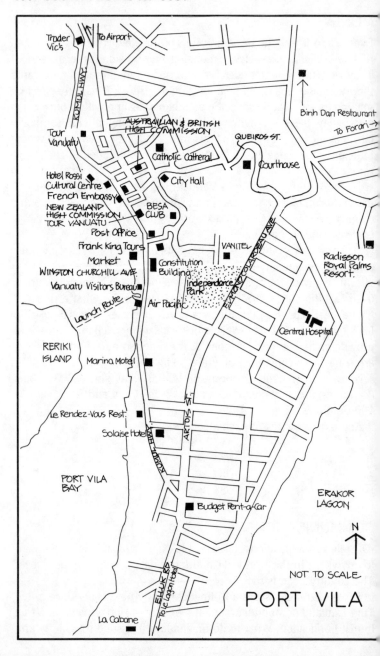

Trader Vic's
To Airport
KUMUL HWY
Binh Dan Restaurant
To Forari →
Tour Vanuatu
AUSTRALIAN & BRITISH HIGH COMMISSION
QUEIROS ST.
Catholic Catheral
Courthouse
Hotel Rossi
Cultural Centre
French Embassy
City Hall
NEW ZEALAND HIGH COMMISSION
TOUR VANUATU
BESA CLUB
Post Office
VANITEL
Radisson Royal Palms Resort.
Frank King Tours
Market
Constitution Building
WINSTON CHURCHILL AVE.
LYCEE COLARDEAU AVE
Independance Park
Vanuatu Visitors Bureau
Launch Route
Air Pacific
RERIKI ISLAND
Marina Motel
Central Hospital
Le Rendez-Vous Rest.
Solaise Hotel
KUMUL HWY
ARTOI ST.
PORT VILA BAY
ERAKOR LAGOON
Budget Rent-a-Car
ELLUK RD
To Le Lagon Hotel
N
NOT TO SCALE
PORT VILA
La Cabane

is available from hotels, tour agencies and some shops.

MISCELLANEOUS

Local time is GMT +11.

Business House
These are flexible. About 7.30 am to 11.30 am, then siesta till 1.30 pm. Shops are open then until 5-7 pm.
Westpac Bank: 8.30 am-3 pm.
ANZ Bank: 8 am-2 pm.
Hong Kong & Shanghai Banking Corp: 8.30 am-11.30 am, 1.30 pm-3.30 pm.
Banque de Indosuez Vanuatu: 8 am-11 am, 1.30-3 pm.

Electricity supply is 220-240 volts, 50 Hz. Plugs are either Australian or French. Adaptors are available at most electrical stores.

Departure Tax is VT1,500 on departing Vanuatu and VT200 for internal flights.

Credit Cards
Diners Club, American Express, Mastercard and Visa are commonly accepted. Bankcard is NOT accepted NOR Australian Bank Credit Cards, if that Bank does not have a branch in Port Vila.

Tipping and bargaining are against Melanesian custom.

Emergency Telephones

Police	2 222
Doctor	2 826
Hospital	2 100
Ambulance	2 100
Dentist	2 306
Fire	2 333
Taxis	2 870

Medical
No vaccinations are required except smallpox and/or yellow fever if entering from endemic areas. Anti-malarial tablets should be taken prior to departure, if visiting the outer islands. The water is safe to drink. There are no poisonous snakes or spiders; however there is a broad-leafed plant with a similar effect to poison ivy.

Port Vila

TRAVEL INFORMATION

HOW TO GET THERE

By Air

Ansett Vila Services, Air Vanuatu, Air Pacific, Air Nauru and Air Caledonie have services from Sydney to Port Vila.

All these airlines offer package deals, such as Ansett Vila Services/Orient Pacific — 7 nights accommodation at the Intercontinental Island Inn plus return economy class airfare from Sydney to Port Vila for $744 per person twin share.

Recently the Government of Vanuatu agreed to allow Norfolk Island Airlines to operate twice weekly charter services between Norfolk Island and Vanuatu.

The international airport is Bauerfield, which is 17 km from Port Vila on the island of Efate. The airport is currently being extended, and when the work is finished it will be able to handle 767 aircraft.

By Sea

Port Vila is a popular port of call for a number of cruise ships, including those operated by P & O, Sitmar, CTC and Royal Viking Lines.

TOURIST INFORMATION

The National Tourism Office is opposite the Burns Philp Store in Port Vila, ph 2 733, 2 745.

ACCOMMODATION

Accommodation can be found on six islands — Efate, Tanna, Espiritu Santo, Bokissa, southern Pentecost and Erromango. Camping is not encouraged in Vanuatu. The only form of camping is at Takara Beach Resort (Efate) where a small fee is payable for tent rental.

Here we have divided Vanuatu hotels and resorts into five categories. Prices are for a double room, and should be used as a guide only.

International

Intercontinental Island Inn, Efate Island (P.O. Box 215), on lagoon edge 3 km from Port Vila, ph 2 040 — VT8,200; Iririki Island Resort, Efate Island (P.O. Box 230) on Iririki Island in Vila Harbour, two minutes by resort's own ferry from waterfront (constant 24 hr service), ph 3 388 — VT8,000; Le Lagon, Efate Island (P.O. Box 86), at the mouth of Erakor Lagoon 3 km from Port Vila, ph 2 313 — VT10,800.

Hotel

Hotel Rossi, Efate Island (P.O. Box 11), has harbour frontage in central Port Vila, ph 2 528 — VT4,755; Olympic Hotel, Efate Island (P.O. Box 709), in central Port Vila, ph 2 464 — VT5,000; Solaise Hotel, Efate Island, rue de Picardie, 5 minutes walk from central Port Vila, also has self-contained accommodation, ph 2 150 — VT4,800 per unit.

Self-contained

Marina Motel, Efate Island (P.O. Box 681), three minutes walk from town centre, ph 2 566 — VT4,750; Vila Chaumieres, Efate Island (P.O. Box 400), 3 km from Port Vila on edge of second lagoon, ph 2 866 — VT5,100.

Getaway

Bokissa Island Resort, opposite town of Luganville on Espiritu Santo Island (P.O. Box 261), ph 2 855 — access is by scheduled Air Melanesiae flight from Vila then 15 minutes by launch to resort — VT6,000.

Manuro Paradise, Efate Island (P.O. Box 1009), 55 km by road from Port Vila, ph 2 378 — VT4,500.

Metesons Guest House, Erromango Island, 30 minutes from Port Vila by Air Tropicana charter flight, or weekly scheduled Air Melanesiae flight, ph 2 219 — VT2,500.

Takara Resort, Efate Island — very basic ocean-front bungalow or tent-rental, ph 3 576 — VT4,200.

Tanna Beach Resort, Tanna Island (P.O. Box 27), 3 km from Tanna Airport — access by twice daily flights from Vila — bungalow accommodation — VT4,400;

White Grass Bungalows, Tanna Island (P.O. Box 5) — access from Vila

Local crafts, French Polynesia

Moorea, French Polynesia

Marquesas, French Polynesia

by scheduled Air Melanesiae flights, bungalow accommodation — VT4,000.

Port Vila Island Resorts

Erakor Island Resort (P.O. Box 24), small island at the mouth of Erakor Lagoon, 3 km by ferry from Port Vila, ph 2 983 — VT4,500. Hideaway Island (P.O. Box 875), small island in Mele Bay, 8 km by ferry and road from Port Vila, ph 2 963 — VT5,600.

LOCAL TRANSPORT

Bus
Buses within Port Vila are VT40 from anywhere to anywhere.

Air
Inter-island transport is mainly by scheduled flights. Charter flights are also available.

Boat
Small inter-island cargo boats mostly carry deck passengers only. Some passenger boats have regular calls through the islands and reservations can be made through your travel agent, or on arrival in Vila at the shipping offices.

Taxi
Taxis are metered by law. They are relatively inexpensive. However when you telephone for one, you will be charged the fare from the depot to the point of collection in addition to the ongoing fare.

Car Hire
Cars, 4WDs, mopeds and bikes are available for hire. Cars drive on the RIGHT hand side.

EATING OUT

Two widely served local delicacies which must be tried during any Vanuatu holiday are coconut crab and flying fox. Both have a naturally rich, "gamey" flavour, which lends itself well to the varied styles of the international brigade of chefs in Vanuatu.

A full list of restaurants, their styles and phone numbers is available from the Information Centre in Port Vila.

Dining out vouchers valid for use in 5 restaurants in Port Vila are available from Walter Tokone of Travel Technology, ·rue Emile

Mercet, Port Vila, ph 3 982. They are priced at A$165 per adult and A$83 per child under 12. The restaurants involved are:

Reflections, Olympic Court, ph 3 639 — coconut crab specialist.

Le Rendez-vous, Main Highway opposite Cine Hickson, ph 3 034 — International.

Tassiriki Inter-Continental Island Inn, on the lagoon, ph 2 040 — different International buffet nightly in the Tuku Tulu Kai Kai, the only BYO restaurant in town.

Harbourview, Main Highway, next to CACB, ph 3 668 — Chinese, in a private house with marvellous views.

Le Pandanas, minutes from the Inter-Continental Island Inn, ph 2 552 — French.

Other vouchers are available for 7 buffet meals at the Inter-Continental Hotel for A$168 per adult, child under 12 free of charge when parents purchase package.

SHOPPING

Port Vila has long been known as a Duty Free Shopping Port for a wide variety of products, ranging from gold and silver jewellery to photo equipment to perfume, watches and fine porcelain.

There is a very large duty-free store in Port Vila, which operates under a new system implemented by the government in September, 1985. Under this system many more products are now available duty free, such as spirits, liqueurs and tobacco; video recorders and audio and video cassettes; compact discs, radio controlled vehicles and a wide range of toys. All sales are made under Customs control to passengers departing both by air and sea. All goods sold can be picked up within two days before departure, and air tickets must be presented at the time of purchase. The articles purchased are packed in specially sealed and labelled bags, and must be hand carried through Customs where the relevant dockets are plucked and retained as proof of export.

The warranties on major brands sold duty free tend to be good.

There are also a number of jewellery stores, souvenir and handicraft outlets and boutiques on Kumul Highway, and in the side streets.

If you're into local handicrafts, shells or colourful pareos, visit the markets in Kumul Highway on Wednesday, Friday or Saturday.

CRUISING

The sea wall at Port Vila is the heart of Vanuatu's cruising community, with both passage-making yachts from all corners of the globe, and local charter boats, moored there.

The wall is adjacent to the local market place and village green, and stretches along to the port's cargo wharves. The warm, clear waters around Vanuatu are an ideal location for the uninitiated to take their first yachting trip. Conversely, it is an equally suitable place for "old salts" to put to sea again.

For dedicated sailors, well-equipped bareboat (non-crewed) yachts are available for charter, while the less experienced have a choice of skippered vessels in a range of sizes and types, from auxiliary cruisers to game fishing or glass-bottom boats.

All boats carry snorkelling gear and some are fully equipped for scuba diving. There is a choice of extended or day charters, and the costs are reasonable.

Regular three day, two night cruises visit the offshore islands to the north of Efate. Departing from Port Vila, it is a good morning's sail around the infamous Devils Point to Havannah Harbour. Rounding the Point was especially difficult for the big square riggers of bygone days, so they had to stay in the bay just behind the Point until the south-east trade winds abated. Their tall masts would warn the locals of their arrival, and the bay is still known as "three masts."

Paul's Rock, a reef just past the Point is not to be missed, if you are an enthusiastic snorkeller.

Hat Island, recognisable by its shape, is north-west of the reef with the entrance to Havannah Harbour, Hilliard Channel, opposite. The island is considered to be sacred by the locals because it is the site of a mass grave, filled when a famous local chief died. It is possible to visit the Island, which is uninhabited, but respect must be shown.

Havannah Harbour is flanked on one side by Efate Island, while the western shores are formed by Lelepa and Moso Islands, with Purumea Pass, a small channel, running between them. There are several villages on these islands, and the surrounding reefs and waters provide excellent snorkelling and fishing. Both Lelepa and Moso Islands have interesting caves to explore, both at sea-level and in the cliffs above. Close to a lagoon are the remains of a WWII anti-aircraft gun base, and a crashed Corsair fighter aircraft.

Beyond Undine Bay the cruising grounds open up with volcanic islands and low coral atolls stretching north. The islands of Emae and Epi can be seen in the distance. The customs on these islands, the thatched huts, the meeting houses, and the people are still untouched by the new ways of Vila, except to rely on the copra boats which call weekly.

Following are a few examples of the companies offering boats for charter.

"Escapade", 13 m cruiser has snorkelling tuition for novices. The Three-Reef-and-Wreck snorkel cruise is very popular. Game fishing and extended charters are available, ph 2071.

Nautilus-Scuba School offers professional teachers who can guide you through reefs and wrecks, and qualify you with an international certificate, P.O. Box 78, Vila.

South Pacific Cruises "Coongoola" is a 23 m live-aboard sailing ship. Offers 3 or 6-day adventure cruises exploring remote islands with all meals and scuba diving inclusive. Sleeps 12 people. P.O. Box 611, Vila.

Yachting World specialises in bareboat and skippered yacht charters. "Julius", a Naut 40 m, and "Magic Moon", a Parreau 34, are available for inter-island sailing holidays, TX 1076.

"Witchitit" sets sail on full-day diving excursions, overnight sailing and spectacular sunset cruises. Contact Nautilus Offshore Charters or Yachting World, Vila, TX 1076.

"Gearra", Island Diver's 13 m ketch specialises in scuba diving, with safe tuition. Contact Richard and Betty below the Pisces Restaurant, ph 2255, P.O. Box 688, Vila.

Dive Action Ltd. also have scuba instruction and guided dives. Group rates are available and special rates on accommodation at Teouma Village Resort, ph 2837/3241, P.O. Box 651, Vila.

Nautilus Scuba was established in 1978 and has fully professional multi-boat operation. Half and full-day charters available. ph 2398, P.O. Box 78, Vila.

1983 — 16 m ketch "Vaimiti" with skipper who is author of "Call of the Sea" and has sailed twice around the world. Day and inter-island charters, and big game fishing. ph 3484, P.O. Box 838, Vila.

"Neptune II", Vila's glass-bottomed fun boat. Cruises three

spectacular reefs. Coral-view, snorkel, hand-feed tame damselfish. Beach barbeque at Paradise Cove included in fare, ph 2272 or 2196, P.O. Box 478.

"Pacific Dream" an 11 m motor cruiser operating in Havannah Harbour. Day trips to Lelepa Island, snorkelling unspoiled reefs. Gordon and Judy Neal, ph 3414, P.O. Box 3413.

SIGHTSEEING

PORT VILA

To familiarise yourself with Vila, take a half-day bus tour arranged by any of the local tourist agencies, such as Travel Technology, rue Emile Mercet, Port Vila, ph 3982, or Frank King Tours in the main street of Port Vila, ph 2808. Or, if you are feeling more adventurous, try catching one of the local buses which for 40 vatu will go to parts of Vila visitors often miss.

Most important is a visit to Vila's Cultural Centre and Museum on Kumul Highway. Here there is a wonderful display of artifacts and photographs. There is also a superb collection of videos on Vanuatu customs.

Next door at "Handicraft Blong Vanuatu", sculptures, wood carvings, basketry and pottery from many of the outer islands, can be purchased.

If modern art is more your forte, visit Michoutouchkine and Pikiolo's art gallery and perhaps buy an original design, hand-painted pareo or shirt. Or visit Acropora coral museum and enjoy a cup of coffee underneath the shade of a pandanus tree.

EFATE ISLAND

There is a lot more to Efate than Port Vila, and "around-the-island" tours are readily available. Alternatively, hire a car or four-wheel-drive and go exploring. Just outside town are a number of fine golf courses and horse riding clubs.

Further on, there is an old manganese mine, magnificent tropical rainforest and friendly villages. Don't hesitate to wander down unmarked dirt roads, as at the end of many are some of Efate's prettiest beaches and scenery.

Eton beach is a favourite stopping place, then on to Takara or Nagar for lunch. From north Efate, on a clear day many of Vanuatu's northern islands can be seen. Visit Siviri village's famous cave where the children "magically" beat the earth to light the inside.

A few miles further on is Havannah Harbour, where the entire US 7th Fleet was stationed during World War II. From Klem's Hill enjoy a magnificent view of Mele Bay, with Port Vila in the background.

Just down the road are Mele's Cascades, where the waters flow all year round.

To see parts of Efate that have remained inaccessible by road, you can arrange a flying tour. The pilot can take you across the island's lush rainforests to the old World War II fighter airstrip at Takara for lunch, then back again that afternoon by a different route. For more information contact the Tourist Information Office.

TANNA ISLAND

The most spectacular attraction on Tanna Island is without doubt Yasur, the "baby" volcano. Because of its size, Yasur is considered one of the safest, most accessible volcanoes in the world. As one vulcanologist put it, Yasur is pleasantly "tame".

As small as it is, it can be quite frightening especially at dusk. The earth shakes and moans and the smell of sulphur permeates the air. Ash clouds drifting to the horizon are dyed burnt orange by the setting sun and the rolling black sand plain around the volcano is tinged with amber. As twilight merges into darkness, the red glow in Yasur's three active vents takes on the more sinister hue of blood red. Then suddenly, Yasur coughs! A spray of lava spears into the night sky and balloons over the edge of the vent like fireworks. The explosive shockwave to follow can be enough to knock over camera tripods, or maybe unsuspecting photographers.

The people of Tanna have never lost their respect for the volcano. Missionaries made their mark here, like everywhere else, but the people are proud of their heritage and are choosing to return to the old ways.

Throughout the year, dozens of ceremonies take place to celebrate special events. Each is spectacular in its own way, but the most amazing is held only once every six or seven years.

The Nekowiar or Toka festival is famed throughout Vanuatu. It is essentially a gift-giving ceremony between villages of mutual clan alliances. The gifts are lap lap (food), kava (narcotic drink) and pigs. The exchange of gifts takes more than three days to complete and during this time the dancing continues virtually non-stop. The rhythmic stomp of a thousand feet shakes the earth almost as much as Yasur. At the end of the Toka over 100 pigs are killed in a sombre, ritualistic manner.

PENTECOST ISLAND

Every year during the months of April and May, the men of southern Pentecost Island leap from tall wooden towers to the ground. The only thing keeping them from death are liana vines tied about their ankles. When missionaries came to the islands, the Nagol or Pentecost Jump vanished from all but one or two villages. In the last few years the people of Bunlap have re-taught the age-old skills to other villages, although even in Bunlap, the origin of the jump is a little hazy.

It seems that a young woman was repeatedly beaten by her husband, Tamalie. She ran deep into the jungle and climbed a coconut tree, hiding in the uppermost fronds. Some time passed before Tamalie found her but as he scaled the tree, she threatened to leap. Ignoring his wife's pleas, Tamalie reached out for her, but she dived to the ground. In a fit of grief (or rage?) he plunged after her to his death, unaware that she had tied vines to her ankles to break her fall.

Every year thereafter, the women of the village tied vines to their ankles and jumped from trees to celebrate the event. Eventually, the ritual altered, as they often do, and it is now the men who leap, not from coconut trees, but from tall towers built around a suitable tree. The Nagol is now associated with the rites of manhood and boys as young as seven jump from lower parts of the tower. In the weeks before the Nagol, each diver must undertake rituals to purify himself and ward off evil spirits during his dive. If the rituals are incomplete, a diver may be injured or killed. Whatever the reason, men have died and injuries are frequent. (This could be a hint for the Kiwis (New Zealanders) in Queenstown who pay for the privilege of jumping.)

The Nagol is also an important part of the yearly yam harvest. As the vines pull taut, each diver's head should just graze the earth, fertilising the soil for that year's yam crop.

The people of Pentecost now invite westerners to watch the Nagol, charging a fee which goes towards community projects. Jump dates are known around six months in advance, and anyone who wishes can fly or sail to the island for the spectacular event.

Irikiki Island Resort, Vanuatu

ESPIRITU SANTO

James A. Michener came to Santo during World War II and was inspired to write "Tales of the South Pacific". Here, too, he found the mysterious island, Bali Hai. The Americans have gone now, but Bali Hai — Ambae Island is its true name — still looks as mystical as ever in the dawn light and Luganville, Santo's only town, has changed little since the war.

There are still quonset huts half buried in the earth and many of the old cinemas stand with cobweb-shrouded movie posters plastered across cracked walls. On the beach, in someone's backyard is a rusted landing barge and just down the way, a US Navy plane sits where it made its last forced landing.

There is a place called Million Dollar Point where the US forces dumped all their war surplus prior to going home. It is an amazing sight. Beach rock has cemented millions of Coca-Cola and 7-Up bottles and bits of machinery into a conglomerate mass stretching over one kilometre.

A short distance away lies the wreck of the "President Coolidge", the largest, most intact and most accessible shipwreck in the world. Outside the channel lies another victim of American-placed mines, the destroyer USS Tucker, its decks now patrolled only by large schools of fish.

Santo is from a time past. People still come from deep within the jungle dressed in traditional gear, to trade for a few basic necessities, then blend quietly back into the shadows.

The island is too quiet for many tourists, but for those with time to ponder on things past, it's like a dream, and for the scuba diver — it's Mecca.

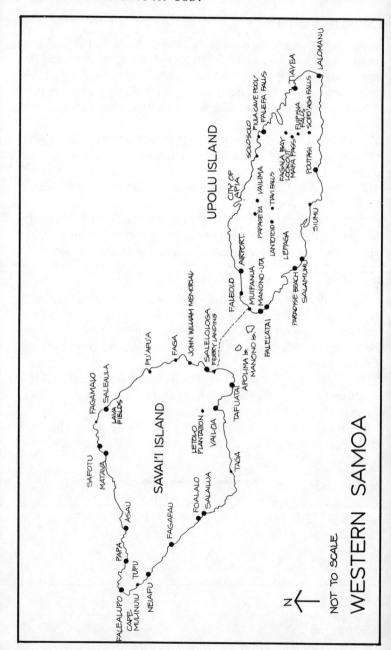

NOT TO SCALE

WESTERN SAMOA

WESTERN SAMOA

Western Samoa, the larger and westerly portion of the Samoan Archipelago, lies 4,216 km (2,614 miles) south-west of Hawaii, 4,355 km (2,700 miles) east of Sydney and 2,903 km (1,800 miles) north-east of New Zealand; Suva, Fiji, is 1,279 km (793 miles) to the west and Pago Pago, American Samoa, only 129 km (80 miles) to the east.

The land area of Western Samoa is 2,850 km^2 (1,100 sq miles) and consists of two main islands, Savaii and Upolu, the smaller islands of Apolima and Manono, and five uninhabited islets. Savaii (1,554 km^2 — 600 sq miles) is the "Big Island", but Apia, the seat of government and centre of commerce, is located on the more populated island of Upolu (1,114 km^2 — 430 sq miles). The islands contain a varied topography ranging from long stretches of white sand beach to lush tropical hardwood forests and 1,835 m (6,000 ft) mountain peaks.

HISTORY

Little is known of the pre-European history of the Samoan Islands, except that Fijians and Tongans conquered and occupied the islands for some time. In 1721, Jacob Roggeveen the first European navigator visited, and in 1768 Frenchman Bougainville anchored, but did not land. The next Frenchman, La Perouse, arrived in 1786, landed, but didn't stay very long as 12 of his crew were killed while searching for water on Tutuila, at a place still called Massacre Bay.

Then in 1791 the English ship the "Pandora" came in search of the mutineers from the Bounty. They were followed by whalers, traders, convicts escaped from Australia, and, of course, missionaries.

The Rev. John Williams of the London Missionary Society landed at Savai'i in 1830 aboard the "Messenger of Peace", and by 1840 most of the Samoans had been converted. The first copra trader in Samoa was John Williams Jr, son of the above.

After the 1830s it was the Germans and Americans who vied to take control of the island group, which was ultimately divided into two, with Germany annexing Western Samoa and the United States exercising sovereignty over Eastern Samoa as a territory under naval control.

During World War I the Germans were driven out by a New Zealand contingent which occupied the islands till 1920. The Treaty of Versailles saw New Zealand receive a mandate that continued until 1946.

World War II did not actively affect Samoa, despite their occupation by Allied troops, and the United Nations gave responsiblity to New Zealand as a trustee for Western Samoa. Measures towards local autonomy were introduced in the 1950s, and the independent State of Western Samoa was created in 1962.

Since independence Western Samoa has enjoyed political stability and economic growth under a parliamentary government which is a unique blend of Polynesian and British practices. The Head of State, whose functions are analogous to those of a constitutional monarch, is chosen from amongst the holders of four chiefly titles. Executive government is carried out by a Prime Minister and the eight Ministers he selects from the 47 member Parliament. There's currently two parties in Parliament: The Coalition Party and the Human Rights Protection Party.

CLIMATE

The climate of Western Samoa is pleasantly tropical 22–30°C (72–86°F) with more than 2,500 hours of sunshine per year. During the sunnier months, May to October, the fresh trade winds make living pleasant and comfortable. Officially the rainy season extends from November through April. In actual fact the pattern is much the same all year round; brief downpours alternate with long stretches of sunshine. Sea temperatures are ideal through the year; mostly around 27°C (80°F) and rarely falling below 24°C (75°F).

POPULATION

There are 162,400 residents (35,000 in Apia) of whom 90% are full Samoans, making this the largest full blooded Polynesian area in the world today. Part Samoans, Europeans, Chinese and other Pacific Islanders make up the remainder of the population.

LANGUAGE

While Samoans pride themselves on their own soft, musical Polynesian language, English is the accepted medium of government and commerce. English is widely spoken in Apia and even in the most remote villages.

Here we have included a few words of Samoan. To help in pronunciation, "go" is pronounced as "ng, and "t" may be pronounced "k. The apostrophe indicates a glottal stop between syllables.

Hello	talofa
Goodbye	tofa
Thank you	faàfetai
Please	faàmolemole
How are you?	faàpefea mai oe?
Where are you going?	alu i fea?
Woman	fafine
Man	tamaloa
House	fale
How much?	pe fia?
Kava bowl	tanoa
Beach	matafaga
Village	nuù
Non-Samoan	palagi
Taboo	sa
Good luck	soifua
Lei	ula
Good night	manuia le po
Beach	matafaga
Boat	vaà
Blowhole	pupu
Very good	lelei tele
Bad	leaga
Yes	ioe
No	leai

PUBLIC HOLIDAYS

January 1	New Year's Day
March/April	Good Friday, Easter Monday
April 25	Anzac Day
June 1–3	Independence Day
December 25	Christmas Day
December 26	Boxing Day

ENTRY REGULATIONS

Visitors must have a valid passport, but no entry permit is required for visits up to 30 days or less. An onward return ticket and indication of a specific place of stay or hotel for accommodation, or where a visitor can be contacted, is required by the immigration authorities.

Written declarations are required for customs. Duty free allowance is one bottle of 40 or 26 oz spirits and 200 cigarettes per person. Firearms, ammunition, explosives, drugs and indecent publications of any kind are prohibited.

It is against the 1950, 1959 and 1960 Laws of Agriculture to import live animals, plants, or products of that nature including fruits, seeds, soil, etc. without authority of the Director.

EMBASSIES

Australia: Australian High Commission, Feagai-Ma-Le-Ata Building, Beach Road, Tamaligi, ph 23 411/2.
New Zealand: NZ High Commission, Beach Road, Apia, ph 21 711.
UK: Honorary British Representative, c/- Armstrong & Springhall (Samoa) Ltd, P.O. Box 498, Apia.
USA: No Resident Representative. Refer to US Embassy in Wellington, NZ, ph 64 (4) 722 068.
Canada: No Resident Representative. Refer to High Commission in Wellington, NZ, ph 64 (4) 739 577.

MONEY

The Western Samoan currency is known as Tala for dollar and Sene for cent (100 sene = WS$1 tala). Foreign currency and travellers cheques are usually accepted at the hotels and at some of the larger stores, and may be exchanged at the local banks during regular business hours.

Approximate rates of exchange are:

A$	=	WS$1.79
NZ$	=	1.35
UK£	=	3.72
US$	=	2.20
Can$	=	1.85

COMMUNICATIONS

The Post Office is open 9 am–4.30 pm Monday–Friday. The Telegraph

Office at the Post Office is open 24 hours every day of the week. Overseas telephone service is available and the Country Code is 685. All calls out of Samoa must be made through the international operator.

The main newspapers are the Observer, the Samoa Times and the Samoa Weekly.

MISCELLANEOUS

Local time is GMT — 11.

Business Hours
Shops: 8 am-12 noon, 1.30-4.30 pm, Mon-Fri. Some stores remain open during the lunch hour.
Banks: 9.30 am-3 pm, Mon-Fri.

Electric current is 240 volts AC50 cycles, but in hotels it is convertible to 110 volts for electric shavers.

There is a departure tax of WS$20.

Credit Cards
Access/Mastercard are accepted on a limited basis. Check with your credit card company for details of merchant acceptability.

Tipping is virtually unknown in Western Samoa and is discouraged.

Mains water is chlorinated, and while relatively safe, may cause mild stomach upsets. Bottled water is available. Drinking water outside main cities and towns may be contaminated, and should be boiled for safety.

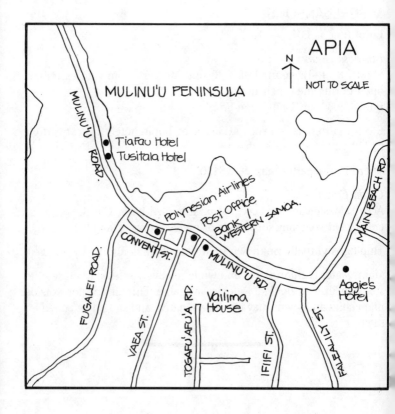

TRAVEL INFORMATION

HOW TO GET THERE

By Air

Faleolo International Airport is serviced by Polynesian Airlines, Air Pacific, Air New Zealand, Air Nauru, South Pacific Island Airways and Hawaiian Airlines. The above airlines have flights from:

Auva — 2 flights a week
Tonga — 2 flights a week
Pago Pago — 6 flights a day
Sydney — 1 flight a week
Auckland — 4 flights a week
Honolulu — 2 direct flights a week, 2 flights via Pago Pago a week.

Airport Transfer —Visitors may reach any hotel from the airport either by airport bus (WS$4) or by taxi (WS$20). Transportation can also be arranged before arrival with a tour operator for a car or bus meeting service for groups or individuals.

By Sea

The following cruise ship lines call at the port of Apia:
CTC Lines, Pacific Far East Lines, Princes Cruises, P & O, Sitmar Cruises and Royal Viking Lines. There are also passenger/cargo ships sailing from Pago Pago to Apia on Tuesday and Thursday, returning on Wednesday and Friday.

TOURIST INFORMATION

Western Samoa Visitors' Bureau, P.O. Box 2272, Apia, ph 20 878. The office is in the Department of Economic Development building on Beach Road, and is open 8 am–12 noon and 1–4.30 pm.

ACCOMMODATION

Following are some examples of the accommodation available. The prices indicated are for a double room per night, and include the 10% government tax. They should be used as a guide only.

Upolu Island

Aggie Grey's Hotel, Vaisigano, (P.O. Box 67, Apia) — on the waterfront at the eastern end of Apia. Agents: Instant Hotels, Australia and New Zealand, HMS International USA — WS$182.

Hotel Tusitala, Apia, (P.O. Box 101, Apia) — international standard — WS$170.

Vaiala Beach Cottages — on Vaiala Beach approx. 1 mile from Apia. Unit accommodation with cooking facilities, ph 22 202 — WS$109.

Harbour Light Hotel — 5 minutes from town near Palolo Marine Reserve, ph 21 103 — WS$50.

Seaside Inn — 5 minutes' walk from Apia Shopping Centre, 1 minute walk from Polynesia Palolo Deep — bed and breakfast accommodation — WS$39.

Betty Moors Accommodation, Matautu — 5 minutes walk to town and to Aggies Hotel — cooking facilities, ph 21 985 — WS$25.

Olivia's Casual Accommodation, Vaiala — adjacent to Apia Park, 5-10 minutes' walk to town — WS$49.

Valentine Parker's Accommodation, Fugalei — 5 minutes' walk to town — rooms with cooking facilities available. Vaiula Beach, on Tafatafa Beach — WS$24.

Savai'i Island

Safua Guest House — 9 thatched "fale" units — meals included.

Amoa Motel, Faga Beach — home-type atmosphere — WS$145 including meals.

Salafai Inn, Salelologa village on eastern tip of Savaii — meals arranged on request — WS$28.

Vaisala Hotel, 15 minutes from Asau Air Strip — 18 self-contained units. ph 21 842 — WS$97.

Taffy's Paradise Beach Inn, Salelologa — close to wharf, Maota Airstrip and central for local buses travelling around Savaii, ph 20 938 — WS$92 including meals.

LOCAL TRANSPORT

Air

Polynesian Airline Internal Service provide flights between Fagalii Airstrip (Apia) or Faleolo Airport on Upolu Island to Asau and Maota

(Salelologa) on Savaii Island. Booking for aerial sightseeing tours and charter flights can be arranged by phoning 21 261 or 22 172.

Ship

The Western Samoa shipping corporation operates daily ferry services between Upolu and Savaii, and a twice weekly service to American Samoa. However because of the frequent schedule changes, it is adviseable to contact Western Samoa Shipping Corporation, Matautu, ph 20 935, or enquire at the Western Samoa Visitors' Bureau for current schedule.

Taxi

Taxi fares are set by the government and published in a pamphlet available at the Visitors' Bureau or the Ministry of Transport Office. The maximum WS$1.20 fare is the one way rate (per 4 passenger taxi) for all rides between the Apia Wharf or any of the Apia Hotels and the centre of the town commercial district (Burns Philp store and the Post Office).

Bus

The public transport buses in Western Samoa are colourful wooden seated vehicles providing inexpensive transportation for local people and the visitor interested in a bit of adventure.

The 30 sene bus fare will take you through the town area or up into the green hills above Apia and through the neighbouring villages and plantations. Usually the maximum rates are about WS$1.60 to the most distant villages and plantations. There are also public buses serving the coastal villages of Savaii Island.

Car

The following companies provide cars for hire:

Pavitt's U Drive, Salenesa Road, Motootua (P.O. Box 290, Apia), ph 21 766; Rainbow Rentals, ph 21 768; Avis, Saleufi St., Apia (P.O. Box 29, Apia), ph 22 468; Hibiscus Rentals, P.O. Box 510, ph 20 162; Budget Rentals, P.O. Box 1602, ph 20 561.

A local driver's licence may be obtained for WS$10 upon producing a driver's licence from another country, or an international driver's licence may be validated for a fee of WS$10 and two passport photos at the Transport division of the Ministry of Transport.

Traffic drives on the left.

EATING OUT

The main hotels provide dining rooms and cocktail lounges for their guests and other visitors. Aggie Grey's, the Tusitala Hotel and Le Godinet's host a Samoan "Fiafia night" once a week. This is an excellent opportunity for the visitor to experience the food and entertainment of Western Samoa. The evening begins with a buffet supper including seafoods such as lobsters, crabs and baked fish in coconut cream. The Samoan stone oven (umu) yields roast suckling pigs, baked taro and taamu, breadfruit and a special Samoan delicacy, palusami (fresh spinach or young taro leaves baked with coconut cream inside banana leaves).

Entertainment includes the traditional dances and songs of Samoa. The guest will have an opportunity to view the graceful siva and the excitement of the Samoan slap knife and fire dances. The evening's programme is rounded out by popular music and dancing. Tour operators will also make arrangements with nearby villages to hold a "fiafia" for cruise ship passengers or other groups of visitors.

Restaurants include Mandarin Palace, Amigos, Love Boat, Canton, Le Godinet, Apia Inn, Treasure Garden, Hotel Tusitala and Aggie's. Enquire at the front desk of your hotel for directions to these restaurants.

In addition to the hotels, those interested in nightlife will find several clubs loosely patterned after western nightclubs, but having a definite island flavour. The Beachcomber, Surfside Pier, Le Bistro, Otto's Reef, Harbour Light Hotel, Mount Vaea, Lafayette's nightclub, Pizza Place (restaurant and bar). The Tusitala Hotel has a live band entertaining from Monday to Saturday at their main bar. A variety of music ranging from the most popular tunes to old favourites, is played by the resident band. Dancing is at the main bar.

SHOPPING

Handicraft

The wide variety of articles made by Samoan families for their personal use are increasingly being sought by visitors because of the beauty of the woods and fibres, the quality of the craftmanship and the uniqueness of the design. Siapo (tapa) cloth made from mulberry bark and painted with native dyes, and mats and baskets of various sizes and weaves are fine examples of traditional crafts. Kava and food bowls are hand carved from the rich native hardwoods. Shell

jewellery and brightly coloured hand-printed fabrics are also popular choices. In Apia, a large selection of local crafts can be viewed and purchased at the government sponsored Handicrafts Store on Beach Road, or from families selling their crafts in the "New Market". Many of the small shops and general stores lining Apia's Beach Road also sell handicrafts. The Philatelic Bureau located at the Post Office, offers a fine selection of Samoan stamps, prized by collectors for their award winning designs. The Treasury Department sells commemorative issues and mint sets of Samoa coins.

Duty Free Shopping

The gift shops at Faleolo Airport (Departure Lounge) have a wide selection of international goods including cigarettes, liquor, perfume, watches, jewellery, electrical goods and gift items.

SIGHTSEEING

Both Upolu and Savaii offer a variety of scenic attractions and places of historical and cultural interest. The visitor staying a week or less will probably concentrate on seeing the many sights of Upolu.

Sightseeing begins soon after arriving at Faleolo Airport, as the 34 km (21 mile) road to Apia winds along the coast past small villages and WESTEC Commercial coconut plantations, giving a close-up view of the life in the island. The drive also passes through some of the newly established industries of the Industrial Estate at Vaitele fronting the main road about five miles from Apia.

Apia retains much of the architecture and charm of its early days as a haven for trans-pacific schooners and a centre of the copra trade. Vailima, the residence of Robert Louis Stevenson or Tusitala (Teller of Tales) as the Samoans called him, is a short ten minutes' drive up through the hills above Apia. When he came to Western Samoa, Stevenson was already a famous writer (Treasure Island, Dr Jekyll and Mr Hyde, etc), and when he died here the residence became the official home of the Head of State. On top of nearby Mt Vaea is Stevenson's Tomb with its immortal "Requiem" carving which reads —

Under the wide and starry sky,
Dig the grave and let me lie.
Glad did I live and gladly die,
and I laid me down with a will.

This be the verse you grave for me:
Here he lies where he longed to be;
Home is the sailor, home from the sea,
And the hunter home from the hill.

Stevenson's wife, Fanny, died in California in 1914. Her ashes were brought back to Samoa and buried at the foot of his grave with a bronze plaque bearing her Samoan name, Aolele, and the words of Stevenson —

Teacher, tender comrade, wife,
A fellow-farer true through life
Heart-whole and soul-free,
The August Father gave to me.

Visitors intending to climb up to the tomb are advised to wear proper shoes as the track is a bit slippery, particularly during the rainy period. The climb takes a few hours, and it is advisable to make it in the morning or evening when it is cooler. Recently the government declared the surrounding area leading up to the tomb as the Tusitala Reserve, which specialises in different species of Samoan woods. A botanical garden has also been started by the National Parks section of the Agriculture Department at the foot of the mountain.

A five minute drive to the west of Apia is the historic Mulinuu Peninsula. This mile long strip of land is the site of the traditional burial grounds of Samoan royalty, the new Parliament House, the Land and Titles Court and the memorial tombs to the foreign naval forces who died in the disastrous hurricane of 1889.

For a full day of touring beyond the Apia area, the 65 km (40 miles) drive along the east coast threads through some of the most colourful scenery in the island, including Piula Cave Pool and Falefa Falls. Then it continues over the Lemafa Pass with its great view of the valley and distant shoreline, past other falls cascading out of the dense foliage, to the beaches and palm-fringed lagoons of the Aleipata district. Here there is an opportunity to see the unspoiled way of life of the people of the outer villages.

Another day trip begins by taking the cross island road towards the south coast through lush green rain forests to the impressive Tiavi Falls. Upon reaching the south-west coast, a stop may be made at Mulivai Beach, which is ideal for swimming and picnicking. Salamumu village, about 5 km (3 miles) from the main road, is a picturesque cluster of thatched roofed houses with a beach just beyond the village. A couple of overseas films have been shot in this village. Nearby Lefaga Bay was chosen as the setting for the filming of Gary Cooper's "Return to Paradise" because of its broad, palm-lined, white sand beach.

At the Western end of Upolu is the Falelatai District, the site of Lefatu Cape where longboats once set off for the neighbouring islands of Manono and Apolima. The largest coconut plantation in the southern hemisphere is located at Mulifanua on the west coast. It is owned by WESTEC, a government corporation involved with bananas, coffee, a soap factory and livestock production.

Savaii, the largest island of the Samoas, lies to the west of Upolu and can be reached in a few minutes by plane, or in one and half hours by boat. Tour operators can arrange a day excursion or a longer visit with lodgings provided in guest fales at Lalomaiva village, about 1.5 hours' drive from Maota Airport in Savaii.

To the north of the Salelologa wharf is the Rev John Williams Memorial, a tribute to the first Christian Missionary who arrived in the Samoas in 1930; the beautiful lagoon at Lano Village, and the massive Lava Fields at Salleaula and Aopo, which were caused by a series of volcanic eruptions in the early 1900s. At the western end of Savaii there are many good swimming beaches, some secluded and others with sites of historical and cultural significance. Vaisala Hotel is located on the northern part of Savaii.

Note: Some villages on Upolu Island, such as Lefaga and Salamumu, charge $1 entrance fee per car to their beaches. Similarly, a fee of $1 is charged at Papaseea Sliding Rocks; $1 per person for Cave Pool at Piula, Fogaafau and Sopoaga Falls.

Tour Agents — Upolu

Gold Star Tours, P.O. Box 185, Apia, ph 20 466 (office in the Goldstar building).
Janes Tour and Travel Ltd., P.O. Box 70, Apia, ph 20 954 (office — Saleufi).
Samoa Scenic Tours, P.O. Box 669, Apia, ph 22 880 (office in Aggie Grey's Hotel).
Retzlaffs Tours, P.O. Box 195, Apia, ph 21 724 (office on Vaea Street).
Trans Pacific Travel, P.O. Box 1176, Apia, ph 21 345 (next door to Goldstar building on Beach Road).
Schuster Tours, P.O. Box 312, Apia, ph 23 014 (contact: Philip Schuster).
Sina Tours, P.O. Box 635, Apia, ph 21 724 (contact: Maraea Slade).
Burns Philp Travel, Beach Road, Apia, ph 22 611.
Union Travel, P.O. Box 50, ph 23 213 (office on Beach Road, Apia).

Tour Agents — Savaii

Vaisala Hotel Tours
Safua Hotel Tours

One of the many natural pools on the islands

RECREATION

Swimming and Diving

Most of the coastline is protected by a reef, and the crystal clear lagoons are ideal for the swimmer or underwater enthusiast.

Vaiala Beach, a quarter of a mile from Aggie Grey's Hotel, has a very strong undertow, especially when the tide is going out or low.

Mulinuu Beach, about one-fifth of a mile from the Hotel Tusitala, is a popular spot with visitors and locals alike.

On the south-west coast there are secluded beaches at Lefaga and Salamumu.

Six miles east of Apia are excellent surfing areas, however swimmers are cautioned to be careful of an undertow during heavy surf.

Palolo Deep on the outskirts of Apia is typical of the hundreds of "deeps" in Samoa's waters, and it ideal for snorkelling, diving and underwater photography.

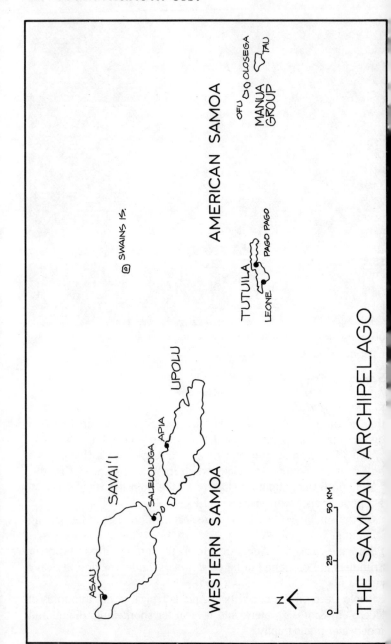

THE SAMOAN ARCHIPELAGO

The mountains and rain forests of Samoa have created a wealth of opportunities for fresh water swimming in the many streams, waterfalls, spring fed pools and lakes. Piula Cave Pool on the East Coast Road, in the grounds of the Methodist Theological College, is a favourite. You could also try Falefa Falls, on the East Coast Road, and Togitogiga Falls on the South Coast.

About five miles from Apia there are the Papaseea Sliding Rocks, which are ideal fun for adults and children.

Golf

At Fagalii, near Apia, is the Royal Samoan Golf Club, site of the Samoa Open Golf Championship in August each year. Visitors are welcome to use the golf course and facilities, and arrangements and payment of green fees may be made through the club secretary at the hotels, or tour agents.

Tennis

Public tennis courts, built for the 1983 South Pacific Games, are in Apia Park, and are open every day from 8am-6pm at $1 per player for half an hour per court.

Private tennis courts at Channel College, Moamoa, are open to visitors on Monday, Wednesday, Saturday and Sunday, ph 21 821 for reservations. The courts at the Tusitala Hotel are for guests only.

Squash

Apia Squash courts are near the Apia Wharf (after Seaside Inn). Enquiries and bookings can be made by phoning 23 780 or 22 571. It also has sauna facilities.

Fitness Centres

Genesis Fitness Spectrum has jazzercise and aerobics classes daily, and weight equipment is available. For more information contact the Visitors' Bureau, or enquire at your hotel desk.

Heems Fitness Centre is located 5 minutes from town and has weight equipment and squash courts, ph 20 182.

Lawn Bowling

The Apia Bowling Club is adjacent to the Hotel Tusitala and Apia Park. Arrangements may be made through the hotels or tour agents.

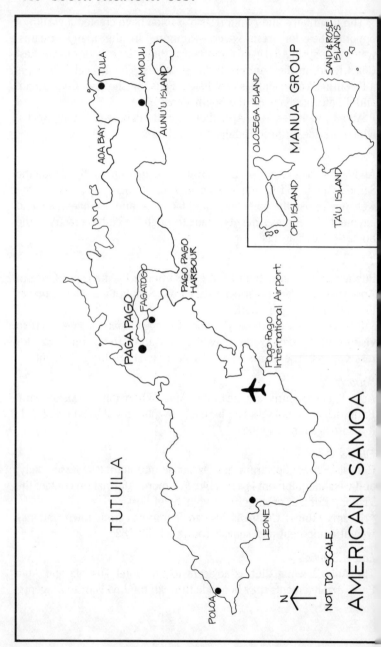

AMERICAN SAMOA

American Samoa is situated in the central South Pacific, 129 km (77 miles) east of Western Samoa, at 13 to 15S and 171 to 173W. It comprises seven islands —

Tutuila, the largest with an area of 137 km² (53 sq miles),
Aunuù,
Manuà Group (Ofu, Oloseag, Taù)
Rose,
Swain's.

The Manuà Group are volcanic in origin, and are dominated by high peaks. Rose and Swain's Islands are uninhabited coral atolls to the east and north respectively of the two island groups.

American Samoa, 3,700 km (2,294 miles) south-west of Hawaii, is the only US Territory south of the equator.

The capital is Pago Pago (pronounced Pango Pango) on the island of Tutuila.

HISTORY

Until 1899 when Germany annexed Western Samoa and the United States took Eastern Samoa, the History section of Western Samoa is common to both.

As Japan began emerging as an international power in the mid-1930s, the US Naval station on Tutuila began to acquire new strategic importance. By 1940, the Samoan Islands had become a training and staging area for the US Marine Corps. It was this massive influx of Americans that — for better or worse — gave Samoans a sudden taste of the benefits of a modern western society.

Fortunately for the islands and for the Samoan people, none of the fighting which scarred so many of the Pacific Islands during World War II ever reached Samoa. In 1945 the Marines left as suddenly as they had arrived, and American Samoa returned to the quiet, peaceful way of life it had enjoyed before that great conflict.

Today, American Samoa is an unincorporated territory of the United States administered by the Department of the Interior. Its people are classified as American nationals. The executive branch of the government is headed by an elected governor and lieutenant governor. American Samoa's Fono — the legislature — is bicameral, with senators chosen by country councils according to Samoan custom and the representatives elected by popular vote. The judicial branch consists of the High Court, the District Court and Village Courts. The head of the judiciary, the Chief Justice, is appointed by the Secretary of the Interior.

CLIMATE

American Samoa's climate is typically tropical, with temperatures seldom exceeding the mid-20s (80s). Nights are balmy and cooling tradewinds blow almost constantly. As in most tropical areas, there are frequent heavy rains but, even during the so-called rainy season (December–March) there are extended periods of bright sunshine on a daily basis. Generally speaking, the weather is sunnier from June through September.

POPULATION

The population of American Samoa is approximately 35,000, of which about 10,000 are Western Samoans, and 3,000 Tongans. Because American Samoans are US nationals, they have free entry to the US and some 60,000 now live in Hawaii and California. As US nationals, not citizens, they can't vote in US presidential elections.

Nearly 70% of high school graduates leave American Samoa for the States within a year of graduation. Although the young have largely forgotten their own culture in their haste to become American, the "faà Samoa" is fiercely defended by those who remain at home.

LANGUAGE

Samoan is the main language, but a large majority speak English.

PUBLIC HOLIDAYS

January 1	New Year's Day
February	Presidents' Day
March/April	Good Friday/Easter Monday
April 17	Flag Day
May	Memorial Day
July 4	Independence Day

July 16	Manuà Flag Day
September	Labour Day
October	Columbus Day
November 11	Veteran's Day
November	Thanksgiving Day
December 25	Christmas Day

The annual celebration of American Samoa's Flag Day in April is a major event with gala traditional ceremonies, a Polynesian longboat race and general re-enactment of the 1900 cession to the United States.

The second Sunday in October is White Sunday, and the children, all dressed in white, take part in a procession to the church, take the seats of honor inside, and lead the service.

Each year in October and November, when the moon and the tide are just right, a sea annelid called the palolo emerges from the reef to begin its annual reproductive cycle. Samoans, who consider the palolo a great delicacy, turn out in force with nets and cheese cloth to scoop up the Caviar of the Pacific, often eating the creatures raw — straight from the water. This is a great opportunity to go native, as thousands of Samoans and visitors alike wade out onto the reef together.

ENTRY REGULATIONS

A passport is required by all, except US citizens, and must be valid for at least 60 days beyond the intended date of departure. No visa is required for either tourist or business visits for stays of less than 30 days, provided a confirmed reservation and documentation for onward travel is held.

The following items may be imported into American Samoa duty free: 200 cigarettes or 50 cigars; 2 bottles of liquor (fifths); a reasonable amount of perfume for personal use.

EMBASSIES

Australia: No resident representative. Refer to High Commission in Western Samoa, ph 665 23 411.

New Zealand: No resident representative. Refer to High Commission in Western Samoa, ph 665 21 711

UK: No resident representative. Refer to High Commission in Canberra, Australia, ph 61 (62) 73 0422.

Canada: No resident representative. Refer to High Commission in Wellington, NZ, ph 64 (4) 739 577.

MONEY

The currency of Western Samoa is the United States Dollar. Approximate exchange rates are:

A$	=	US$0.82
NZ$	=	$0.62
UK£	=	$1.70
Can$	=	$0.85

COMMUNICATIONS

International telephone calls are available, and the Country Code is 684.

The Post Office in the Lumanaì Building in Fagatogo is open 24 hours. There are also branches in Leone and Faguita villages open 8 am–4 pm Mon–Fri, and 8.30 am–12 noon Saturday.

Publications include the Samoa Journal, the Samoa News, and the South Seas Star. There is a Samoan and English radio station and a public television station. Three channels of television viewing are available during the evening hours until 12 midnight.

MISCELLANEOUS

Local time is GMT — 11.

Business Hours

Banks: 9 am–3 pm Mon–Fri. Bank of Hawaii and Amerika Samoa Bank offer a special service window open until 4.30 pm Friday. Amerika Samoa Bank, Nuùuli Branch is open Saturday 9am–12 noon.

Shops: 8am–5 pm Mon–Fri, 8am–1 pm Sat.

Electric current is 110/120 volts AC, 60 cycles.

There is no departure tax.

Credit Cards are widely accepted.

Although this is an American territory, tipping is not encouraged.

The Fagàlu Institution offers 24 hour medical and dental service, and there is full health care available at the LBJ Tropical Medical Centre

Pago Pago bay with the Rainmaker Hotel in the foreground and the mountain with the same name forming a backdrop

DO'S AND DONT'S

*When visiting a village, ask before snapping photos, picking flowers, using the beach, etc. Each Samoan thinks of the entire village as his own. Permission will almost certainly be granted.

*In a Samoan home, sit before talking or eating. When seated, try to fold your legs under you. It's considered impolite to stretch your legs straight out in front of you.

*If you should be honoured with a request to share kava with Samoans, spill a few drops on the ground or mat in front of you before drinking.

*Don't eat while walking through a village.

*Every evening at dusk, each Samoan village takes about 10 minutes for family prayers. If you are passing through the village on foot, you should stop and wait quietly. Or, if invited to join in prayer with a family, do so by all means if you wish. If you are passing through the village by car during this brief evening period, simply continue on your way.

*It's thoughtful to be extra quiet on Sundays.

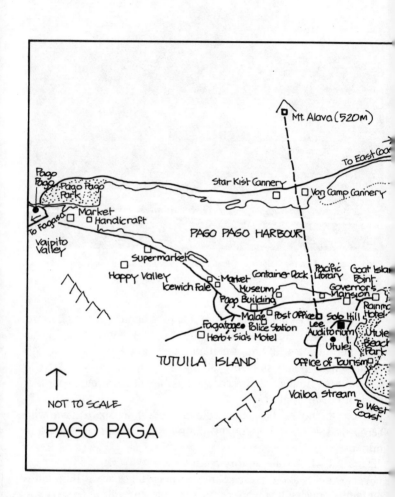

TRAVEL INFORMATION

HOW TO GET THERE

By Air

Hawaiian Airlines have flights from Los Angeles, San Fransicso and Las Vegas, via Honolulu to Pago Pago.

South Pacific Island Airways flies to Pago Pago from Hawaii, Apia and Tonga.

Polynesian Airlines have services from Apia, Rarotonga and Tahiti. Pago Pago International Airport is at Tafuna, 11 km (7 miles) south-west of Fagatogo, ph 699 9906.

By Sea

The following passenger lines call at Pago Pago: Sitmar, Princes Cruises, P & O, Pacific Far East Line and Chandris.
The port is also served by passenger/cargo lines: Polynesian Shipping, Union Steamship, China Navigation, and Farrell Line.

TOURIST INFORMATION

Tourist Information Office is in the Convention Centre near the Rainmaker Hotel, open Mon–Fri, 7.30 am–4 pm. Office of Tourism, P.O. Box 1147, Pago Pago, American Samoa 96799, ph 699 9280.

ACCOMMODATION

For people seeking inexpensive or a more personal form of accommodation in American Samoa, the "Fale, Fala ma Ti" (house, mat and tea) offers such a service. The Fale, Fala ma Ti provides a cross between guest and host in the villages which are located either near the coastal areas or further inland. The host acts as unofficial authority on the islands, offering information on the Samoan way of life, customs and traditions.

Accommodation varies from US$10 to US$25 depending on the homes. Some are Western styled homes, others are the typical thatched roof fales or a Samoan "faletalimalo" (guest house). There is also available space for campers on a private beachhome. All of the

Pago Pago harbour

homes have modern conveniences, additional provisions will require extra cost.

Visitors interested in the FFT should make prior arrangements with the Office of Tourism, or for further information ph 633 5187 or 633 5188.

On the western side of Tutuila, there is the Apiolefaga Inn, a twenty-four room establishment, full bar and a swimming pool. Transportation is provided to anywhere on the island, and they will arrange private tours. P.O. Box 336, Pago Pago, ph 699 9124.

At the other end of the scale is The Rainmaker Hotel, which is of international standard, with everything you expect, such as bars, lounges, dining rooms, coffee shop, etc. Accommodation is in newly renovated air-conditioned rooms in the main building, or luxurious fales on the hotel's private beach — standard US$60, superior US$72, de-luxe US$85, suite US$125 (subject to change). For reservations and information contact the hotel, ph 633 4241/4033 — P.O. Box 996, Pago Pago, American Samoa, 96799.

There are also motels on Tutuila and the Manuà Islands.

LOCAL TRANSPORT

Bus
There is a service from the airport to the centre of Pago Pago, and an unscheduled service connecting Fagatogo and the outlying villages.

Taxi
There is no shortage of taxis, and the fares are fixed by the government.

Ship
There are services between Pago Pago and the Manuà Islands, and around the island of Tutuila calling at the coastal villages. Contact the Tourist Information Centre for further information.

An inter-island boat operates between American Samoa and Western Samoa, twice weekly. The trip to Apia, Western Samoa, takes about six to eight hours.

Car
There are local car rental companies which require drivers to be at least 25 years of age, and Avis and Hertz whose minimum hiring age is 21. Driving is on the right hand side of the road.

EATING OUT

The restaurant and snack bar at the Rainmaker Hotel offer a good selection of fare from hamburgers to authentic Samoan food. The hotel offers a very popular Mongolian Barbecue once a week.

The Rainmaker Hotel, Herb & Sia's Motel and Apiolefaga Inn present a fiafia, or Samoan feast, complete with traditional dancing, on a designated night.

Samoan village fiafias can be arranged through the local tour operators. These include a kava ceremony, authentic Samoan food such as roast pig, breadfruit, taro and puiasami, made from coconut cream wraped in taro leaves and cooked in the umu or ground oven.

An array of restaurants and fast food establishments dot the island and provide a variety of ethnic favourites such as American, Chinese, Japanese, Mexican, Italian and Polynesian. Listed by area, they include:

Fagatogo

Ala Moana Recipe; Big Jake's, Caesar's Restaurant and Lounge; Hot Dog City, Ice-wich Fale; Kim's Restaurant; Milovale's Drive-In; Shimasaki; Teo's Kitchen; Mike Bird's.

Pago Pago

Foremosa Restaurant; Evalani's; Park Fast Food Outlets; Soli's & Mark's Family Restaurant; Leo's Fast Food.

Utulei

Ala Moana Recipe; Shimasaki.

Nu'uuli

A & A Pizza; Matai's Pizza Fale; Milovale's Drive-In; Hot Dog City; Pete's Laundromat.

Tafuna (Airport)

Airport Restaurant; Pete's.

Malaloa

Korean Bar B-Q.

Fagaalu (Hospital)

Lydia's Snack Bar.

Lepuapua

Pita's Drive-In.

Leloaloa

Ramona Lee Restaurant.

Atu'u (across from Samoa Packing)

Teò Fuavai's Place.

Malaeimi (across from ASCC)

Anacleto's.

There are also quite a few nightspots, all of which have that time-honoured American custom of the Happy Hour, between 4.30 and 6.30 pm.

SHOPPING

The Rainmaker Hotel has a duty free shop, and there is another branch of the same firm near the hospital.

Near the end of the harbour is the Senior Handicraft Market, which has all the usual — tapa cloth, shells, basketry, etc.

South Pacific Traders, at Tafuna near the airport, is the largest department store.

SIGHTSEEING

Pago Pago harbour is the crater of an extinct volcano. It was the setting for Somerset Maugham's short story "Rain", which featured Sadie Thompson, and was made into a classic Hollywood movie starring Rita Hayworth.

Mount Alava Aerial Tramway, 1.5 km long, runs from Solo Hill, above Government House, across Pago Pago Bay, to the summit of Mount Alava (488 m — 1,596 ft). It is a breathtaking ride along one of the world's longest non-supported cable spans, and excellent views can be enjoyed in every direction from an observation point on the summit. The clearest views are in the early morning and the late afternoon. The tramway is open every day except Sunday, from 8 am–4 pm, and there is a small charge.

The Jean P. Haydon Museum, Fagatoto, has changed little since it was built in 1917. Originally constructed to serve as the Naval Base Commissary, it accommodated the central Post Office for 20 years. Now housing the territorial museum, it bears the name of its founder in appreciation of her dedication towards its successful completion. Artifacts, handicrafts and items of cultural history are on display.

In front of the museum entrance are Samoan fales. From these authentic Samoan houses, natives offer a variety of local arts and crafts demonstrations.

Nearby is the Fono (Legislature) building. This new structure demonstrates a successful blending of traditional architecture and modern materials. Both the fale tele (round meeting house) and the fale afolau (long oval-shaped residence) designs are incorporated in the structure.

The Courthouse of American Samoa, a stately, white two-storey building, cost $46,000 and was completed in four years. It more closely resembles a Southern mansion than a government building, and was used during the Navy administration to house the offices of the Commandants, the Governor, and the Attorney General. In addition, chiefs, leaders and representatives of the various villages throughout the territory have used the structure as a meeting place.

Alfono Pass, which winds from one side of Tutuila to the other, offers seven scenic points from which Pago Pago Harbour and the north shore of the island can be viewed.

Aasu (Massacre Bay) is where the murder of 11 members of a French Scientific Expedition in 1787 shocked the Western world and precluded those governments from establishing themselves on Tutuila until the late 19th century. To this day, French warships return to Aasu to honour their fallen comrades.

Blunt's Point, a gun emplacement during World War II, Breaker's Point, Virgin Falls and Leone Falls are just a few highly recommended scenic spots considered "must-sees" for the first-time visitor.

Another favourite place for locals and visitors alike is Vaitogi Village, around which a very special story revolves. According to legend, a young married couple who were very much in love learned that the husband was designated for the feast of the cannibal king Malietoa Faiga. Fearing reprisals on their village, they set out for the island of Upolu. Their canoe was blown off course and they were carried to Tutuila where they were offered lodging in the home of the generous Chief Letuli of Ili'ili.

Later, when King Malietoa ceased to practise cannibalism, the

Letuli family offered to escort the couple back home. They refused, wanting instead to repay the chief and his family for their kindness. Together they climbed a cliff in Vaitogi and jumped into the sea. Instantly, the husband turned into a shark and his wife became a turtle. The shark told the villagers, "If you wish us to appear on the surface of the sea, let the children stand on the cliff and sing." To this day, children still assemble on the rocks, and when they sing, it is said, a huge shark and turtle appear on the surface.

MANU'A ISLANDS

At the easternmost end of the Samoan archipelago lie the Manu'a Islands, a relatively undisturbed and strongly culture-oriented part of American Samoa.

Located on the islands of Ofu, Olosega, and Ta'u, and with a total population of 3,500, are the villages of Ofu, Olosega, Sili, Fitiuta, Faleasao, Si'ufaga and Lume. The twin villages of Si'ufaga and Luma, also known as Ta'u village, were the site of Margaret Mead's anthropological study which resulted in her book, "Coming of Age in Samoa".

A great majority of original history, legends and stories, which make up the basis of oral traditons and formal ceremonies of the Samoans, are based on incidents that occurred on Ta'u, believed to be ancient Samoa.

Whether the first Polynesians lived in Manu'a or Savai is still a matter of conjecture. It is conceded, however, that the Tuimanu's (King of Manu'a) was, in fact, one of the strongest and most powerful leaders of ancient Samoa and neighbouring islands. It is commonly believed that holders of the Tuimanu's title held both supernatural and human powers.

A visit to Manu'a will reveal many fascinating living examples and tangible evidence of the ancient legends and stories of Samoa.

INDEX